Object Lessons
Based on Bible Characters

Object Lessons Series

Bess, C. W., *Object-Centered Children's Sermons*, 0734-8

Bess, C. W., *Sparkling Object Sermons for Children*, 0824-7

Bess, C. W., & Roy DeBrand, *Bible-Centered Object Sermons for Children*, 0886-7

Biller, Tom & Martie, *Simple Object Lessons for Children*, 0793-3

Bruinsma, Sheryl, *Easy-to-Use Object Lessons*, 0832-8

Bruinsma, Sheryl, *New Object Lessons*, 0775-5

Bruinsma, Sheryl, *Object Lessons for Every Occasion*, 0994-4

Bruinsma, Sheryl, *Object Lessons for Special Days*, 0920-0

Bruinsma, Sheryl, *Object Lessons for Very Young Children*, 0956-1

Claassen, David, *Object Lessons for a Year*, 2514-1

Connelly, H. W., *47 Object Lessons for Youth Programs*, 2314-9

Coombs, Robert, *Concise Object Sermons for Children*, 2541-9

Coombs, Robert, *Enlightening Object Lessons for Children*, 2567-2

Cooper, Charlotte, *50 Object Stories for Children*, 2523-0

Cross, Luther, *Easy Object Stories*, 2502-8

Cross, Luther, *Object Lessons for Children*, 2315-7

Cross, Luther, *Story Sermons for Children*, 2328-9

De Jonge, Joanne, *More Object Lessons from Nature*, 3004-8

De Jonge, Joanne, *Object Lessons from Nature*, 2989-9

Edstrom, Lois, *Contemporary Object Lessons for Children's Church*, 3432-9

Gebhardt, Richard, & Mark Armstrong, *Object Lessons from Science Experiments*, 3811-1

Godsey, Kyle, *Object Lessons About God*, 3841-3

Hendricks, William, & Merle Den Bleyker, *Object Lessons from Sports and Games*, 4134-1

Hendricks, William, & Merle Den Bleyker, *Object Lessons That Teach Bible Truths*, 4172-4

Loeks, Mary, *Object Lessons for Children's Worship*, 5584-9

McDonald, Roderick, *Successful Object Sermons*, 6270-5

Runk, Wesley, *Object Lessons from the Bible*, 7698-6

Squyres, Greg, *Simple Object Lessons for Young Children*, 8330-3

Sullivan, Jessie, *Object Lessons and Stories for Children's Church*, 8037-1

Sullivan, Jessie, *Object Lessons with Easy-to-Find Objects*, 8190-4

Trull, Joe, *40 Object Sermons for Children*, 8831-3

Object Lessons
Based on Bible Characters

William C. Hendricks

BAKER BOOK HOUSE
Grand Rapids, Michigan 49516

Published by Baker Books
a division of Baker Book House Company
P.O. Box 6287, Grand Rapids, MI 49516-6287

ISBN: 0-8010-4373-5

Fifth printing, March 1998

Printed in the United States of America

For information about academic book, resources for Christian leaders,
and all new releases available from Baker Book House, visit our web
site:

http://www.bakerbooks.com/

Contents

1. **Adam** Genesis 2:18 8
God is concerned about our loneliness
2. **Enoch** Genesis 5:24a 11
Walking with God
3. **Noah** Psalm 22:7–8a 13
Laughing for the wrong reasons
4. **Abraham** Genesis 12:1 15
Obedience—because I told you so
5. **Lot** Genesis 13:12b 17
Protection against evil
6. **Lot's Wife** Genesis 19:26 19
Think more of obeying God than of things you have
7. **Isaac** Genesis 22:2 21
God wants us to love him most of all
8. **Esau** Mark 8:36 24
Choose the most important things
9. **Jacob** Genesis 28:16 27
God is everywhere
10. **Joseph** Genesis 50:20 30
God always has control over our lives
11. **The Cupbearer of King Pharaoh** Genesis 40:23 32
Forgetting to do good
12. **Miriam** Exodus 2:4, 7 34
Loving and caring for brothers and sisters
13. **Moses** Numbers 20:10b–11a 37
Anger can lead to trouble
14. **Aaron** Psalm 141:2 39
God desires and is pleased with the prayers of his children

15. **Joshua** — Joshua 24:15c — 42
    Christian families
16. **Caleb** — Numbers 13:23b — 44
    Believing God's promises
17. **Achan** — Joshua 7:21 — 47
    Coveting can lead to other sins
18. **Gideon** — Judges 6:37 — 50
    Searching for God's will in our lives
19. **Samson** — Judges 14:14 — 53
    For real strength you must depend on God
20. **Ruth** — Ruth 1:16b — 56
    Choose to be with God's people
21. **Samuel** — 1 Samuel 3:9b — 58
    Listening to God
22. **King Saul** — 1 Samuel 10:22–24 — 61
    God honors those who are humble
23. **David** — 1 Samuel 17:45 — 64
    Defending the honor of God's people
24. **Solomon** — Proverbs 6:6 — 67
    Learning helpful proverbs
25. **Elijah** — 1 Kings 19:4b — 70
    Our strength to face trouble comes from God
26. **Elisha** — 2 Kings 6:6b, 16 — 73
    God is all-powerful and everywhere
27. **Naaman's Servant Girl** — 2 Kings 5:3 — 75
    Every Christian has an important mission
28. **Nehemiah** — Nehemiah 2:2 — 78
    Happiness shows on your face
29. **Haman** — Esther 6:6b; 7:10 — 81
    Pride is like a soap bubble that bursts
30. **Job** — Job 2:10b — 84
    God may choose to send us bad as well as good things
31. **Jeremiah** — Jeremiah 18:6 — 87
    God has power over all people and nations
32. **Daniel** — Daniel 6:11, 16 — 90
    The importance of prayer
33. **Jonah** — Jonah 1:3 — 92
    Going the right way

34. **John the Baptist**   Matt. 3:1–2; Acts 11:26c   94
    It means something to be called a Christian
35. **Philip**   John 1:46b   97
    Bringing others to Jesus
36. **Nathanael**   John 1:48   99
    Jesus sees us wherever we are
37. **The Boy with Five Loaves and Two Fish**   John 6:9   101
    The importance of sharing
38. **The Woman Who Touched Jesus' Robe
    and Was Healed**   Mark 5:28   104
    Having faith in Jesus
39. **Zacchaeus**   Luke 19:10   107
    Jesus came to seek and to save the lost
40. **Thomas**   John 20:27   109
    Proof of Jesus' resurrection
41. **James the Son of Alphaeus**   Matthew 10:3   111
    Silent followers of Jesus
42. **Simon the Zealot**   Matthew 10:4   113
    Being enthusiastic for God's kingdom
43. **Pontius Pilate**   Matthew 27:24   115
    Only Jesus' blood can cleanse us from sin
44. **Ananias and Sapphira**   1 Samuel 16:7b   118
    God knows all of our thoughts
45. **Stephen**   Acts 7:60   121
    Forgiving others
46. **The Apostle Paul**   Mark 16:15   123
    Although we give away the gospel, we still keep it
47. **King Agrippa**   Acts 26:28   125
    Being "almost" a Christian is not enough
48. **Eutychus—the Young Man Who Slept
    in Church**   Matthew 13:9   127
    Attentiveness in church
49. **Dorcas**   Acts 9:39b   130
    Showing love for Jesus by helping others
50. **Timothy**   2 Timothy 1:5   132
    It's a blessing to belong to the family of God

1

Adam

Concept: God is concerned about our loneliness

Object: A large cutout number 1

Text: Genesis 2:18

The LORD God said, "It is not good for the man to be alone. I will make a helper suitable for him."

Who knows what number this is? (*Hold up the cutout number 1. Allow responses.*) Right! And the next number is two, and then comes three. Some of you can probably count much farther than that! How many of you can count to 100? (*Allow responses.*) Some of you can probably count farther than 100—maybe even to 1,000. Did you know that even if you counted all of your life you would never get to the biggest number?

People who study numbers tell us that the line of numbers is infinite—it goes on and on and doesn't end. That means if you think you know the biggest number, it really isn't the biggest number after all because you can always add one more to it.

Long, long ago, when God created Adam, you could have used just this number (*hold up your large number 1*) to count all of the people on earth because there was only one. Adam was all alone. He didn't have any other person to talk to or be with.

How do you feel when you are all alone? Maybe you feel alone when you are in your bedroom and your mom goes down to the basement or outside and you don't know where she is. Maybe you feel alone when your dad and mom are at work and no one is at home when you come home from school. Do you know what it feels like to be all alone?

There are many people in the world who sometimes feel very much alone. Children can feel alone when they start a new school. Families can feel alone when they start going to a new church. Old people can feel alone if they are sick or in a nursing home and nobody comes to visit them.

Long ago Adam was the only person on earth. God cared about Adam's loneliness. Then God did a wonderful miracle—he created Eve so that Adam would not be alone anymore.

God still cares when his children are lonely. He promised that he would never leave us. That means we are never really alone because God is always near us.

We need to do all we can to help lonely people, too. How can we do that? There are many ways.

If you see somebody in church school who doesn't have any friends, maybe you could say "Hi" and be friends with that person.

If you haven't seen your grandpa or grandma for a long time, maybe you could send them a letter. Your mom or dad may have other ideas about ways to help people who feel lonely.

God created Eve so that Adam would no longer be all alone. Did you know that Jesus suffered in the Garden of Gethsemane and died on the cross all alone for us so that we could be friends with God? We can show him how thankful we are by being friends to others who are lonely too. Let's try.

2

Enoch

Concept: Walking with God
Object: A walking shoe
Text: Genesis 5:24a

Enoch walked with God.

Do you know what this is? *(Hold up the walking shoe. Allow responses.)* Yes, it's a shoe, but it's a special kind of shoe. When I bought it, I told the clerk in the shoe store that I needed a good "walking shoe." This is one of my walking shoes.

Walking is good for you. It gives you exercise; your lungs breathe in more fresh air and your heart stays strong because it has to pump the blood to your muscles.

It's always nice to walk with someone. While you walk along together, you can talk about all kinds of things. It's nicer to walk and talk with someone you agree with than to walk with someone you are always arguing or quarreling with.

Long ago, before God sent the flood on earth to destroy all the wicked people who lived at that time, there lived a man who loved God. The Bible says that he walked with God. The name of that man was Enoch.

Did you know that you can walk with God like Enoch did? You can. You can because God is everywhere. He is always close beside you, but you have to remember that he is there with you. "Walking with God" means that you walk in the way that he wants you to go. It means that you try to obey his commandments.

You can always talk to him, too. When we pray we are talking to God. God is always ready to hear and answer our prayers.

Enoch must have enjoyed walking with God. God must have loved Enoch very much because he took Enoch home to heaven.

What can we learn from Enoch? Well, boys and girls, we can learn to walk with God like Enoch did. Let's try to remember that God is always with us.

3

Noah

Concept: Laughing for the wrong reasons
Object: Sign with words HA, HA and laughing
faces on it
Text: Psalm 22:7–8a

*All who see me mock me; they hurl insults, shaking their
heads: "He trusts in the LORD; let the LORD rescue him."*

Do you know what this sign says? *(Hold up the HA,
HA sign. Allow responses.)* That's right. The sign says
HA, HA—the words we sometimes say when we
laugh. Do you like to laugh? *(Allow responses.)* Good!
Most people do. What kinds of things make you
laugh? *(Allow responses.)*

Long ago, many people laughed at a man in the
Bible whose name was Noah. At that time all the
people living on the earth were very wicked except
Noah and his family. They were the only people who
loved and obeyed God.

Then God told Noah to build an ark because God
was going to send a flood to destroy the earth. And
Noah did what God told him to do.

What do you suppose the wicked people did when
they saw Noah building the ark? *(Point to the HA, HA
sign.)* Yes, they laughed. They didn't believe in God.

They didn't believe that God would send a flood, and they laughed at Noah for doing what God wanted him to do.

It's no fun getting laughed at, is it?

Did you know that today when Christians really try to obey God like Noah did, other people who don't believe in God, and think that obeying God is foolish, may still laugh at them?

Did anyone ever laugh at you because you tried to be good and obey God? Or, did you ever laugh at someone else who was really trying to be good and obey God?

We can learn at least two things from Noah and the people who laughed at him when he obeyed God. Listen carefully and let's try to remember them both:

1. Don't worry if others laugh at you when you try to do what God wants you to do.
2. Don't laugh at others who are trying to do what God wants them to do.

4

Abraham

Concept: Obedience—because I told you so
Object: A road map
Text: Genesis 12:1

The LORD had said to Abram, "Leave your country, your people and your father's household and go to the land I will show you."

This is a road map, girls and boys. *(Show girls and boys the road map.)* How many of you have seen one of these? *(Allow responses.)* When do your moms and dads use a road map? *(Allow responses.)*

A road map shows us where we live. *(Point out name of city where you live.)* _____ is right here on the map. And here is _____. *(Point out a nearby city or several places known to the children.)*

When you go on a trip, a road map helps you to find where you are going. It shows the best roads to take and how far you will have to travel.

The Bible tells us about a man named Abraham who lived long ago. Abraham and his wife, Sarah, lived in the land of Ur of the Chaldees where all their friends and family members lived.

One day God called Abraham and said,

"Leave your country, your people and your father's house-hold and go to the land I will show you."

God didn't give Abraham a road map, and he didn't tell Abraham how far away this land was.

Abraham didn't say, "Well, God, I can't go because I don't know the road and I don't know how many miles I have to travel." Abraham didn't even ask, "Why, God? Why must I go away from here?" No; Abraham believed that God would lead and guide him to the land where God wanted him to be.

Sometimes our moms or dads tell us to do something and we ask, "Why?" Sometimes they give us a reason and sometimes they just say, "Because I told you so, that's why."

We can't always understand why we need to do what our parents ask us to do, and we can't always understand why we need to do what the Bible tells us to do, but we still must obey. Our heavenly Father tells us to "Honor our father and mother." He doesn't say we have to understand everything first before we obey them.

When God called Abraham to go to a faraway country, Abraham obeyed God even though he didn't understand all the reasons. God blessed Abraham for his faith and obedience.

Remember that God will still bless his children today when they trust him and obey him even though they don't know or understand all the reasons why.

5

Lot

Concept: Protection against evil
Object: Suntan or sun screen lotion
Text: Genesis 13:12b

Lot lived among the cities of the plain and pitched his tents near Sodom.

How many of you know what causes sunburn? *(Allow responses.)* What should you do before you go out to play in the bright sunshine? *(Show the girls and boys the suntan or sun screen lotion you have. Allow responses.)* Right. That's really a good idea because suntan or sun screen lotion keeps you from getting sunburned.

If you don't put on suntan or sun screen lotion, you can get burned so that it really hurts. Getting sunburned usually happens so slowly that you hardly notice it's even happening at all. You just go out in the sunshine and gradually, while you are playing, your skin gets redder and redder; then all of a sudden you notice how badly you got sunburned.

Then it's too late. You got burned so slowly you didn't notice that it happened. But now it hurts.

Doing things that are wrong sometimes gets started the same way. First you do a few wrong things. Then gradually, before you know it, you are doing more and more wrong things.

That's what happened to a man in the Bible named Lot. Lot and his Uncle Abraham had many flocks of sheep. When there wasn't enough grass in one place for all the sheep to eat, Abraham and Lot decided to go to live in different places.

Lot chose to go toward the cities of the plains, the evil cities of Sodom and Gomorrah. First Lot just looked toward the cities. Then he set up his tents near them. Then he got closer still; he went to the city gates. Finally he and his family actually lived *in* the evil cities.

Gradually Lot got closer to the evil of the cities. It probably happened as slowly as getting sunburned.

Then God sent his angel to destroy these evil cities. Lot and his family barely got out alive.

When you live close to sin, you gradually get used to it, like Lot did. That's worse than getting sunburned because you can't put on sun screen lotion to protect yourself. One of the best things is to get away from the sin. That's just like coming in out of the sun. But if you can't get away from the sin, the best screen you can use is the screen of reading the Bible and praying. The closer you live to God and his Word, the less likely it will be that you get burned with the sin that is all around you.

Every time you put on suntan or sun screen lotion, think about how we all need God's screen to keep us away from evil things.

Lot's Wife

Concept: Think more of obeying God than of things you have

Object: A cup of salt in an open dish

Text: Genesis 19:26

But Lot's wife looked back and she became a pillar of salt.

What do you think this is, girls and boys? *(Show the girls and boys your dish with a small pile of salt in it. Pick up a small amount of salt between your fingers and let it run back down into the dish.)* Yes, it looks like it could be either salt or sugar. How can we tell which one it really is? *(Allow responses.)* If I taste it *(do so, or perhaps have an eager child moisten a finger and try a little),* I can tell if it's really salt or sugar. Yes, it really is salt.

Salt helps us in many ways. It makes our food taste better and it helps to keep food from spoiling. Our bodies need a little bit of salt to keep us healthy too. I guess that's why God made salt when he created the world.

In the Bible, in the Book of Genesis, there is a story about salt. The story really started when the servants who cared for Lot's flocks and herds and the servants who cared for Abraham's flocks and herds both wanted the same pasture land for their animals. Because of this, Lot and his family started moving toward the wicked cities of Sodom and Gomorrah.

Slowly Lot and his family moved closer to these wicked cities until they lived right in them. God came to punish these cities for the wicked things they did. But before he destroyed the cities, God sent his angels to save Lot and his family.

The angels took Lot and his wife and daughters and led them out of the city. The angels said, "Run away to the mountains, flee for your lives, and don't look back!" Lot's family had to leave their house and all of the nice things in it.

Lot's wife didn't do what God wanted her to do. Instead of obeying the angel of God, she *did* look back to see what would happen to all of the things she owned.

The angel of God had said, "Don't look back!" but she did, and God punished her for not being obedient. She turned into a pillar of salt. *(Let some of the salt run through your fingers again.)*

I can't make this salt stand up in a little pillar. It just sinks down into the dish. When God changed Lot's wife into a pillar of salt it was a miracle, and only God can do miracles.

It's a strange but important story. It teaches us that God wants us to obey him, and we should not think more of the things we have than we do of obeying him. So the next time you use salt, think of Lot's wife and remember that God wants us to obey him and to love him more than anything else.

7

Isaac

Concept: God wants us to love him most of all

Objects: A test paper or test form and a pencil

Text: Genesis 22:2

Then God said, "Take your son, your only son Isaac, whom you love, and go to the region of Moriah. Sacrifice him there as a burnt offering on one of the mountains I will tell you about."

Have you or your older brothers or sisters ever had to take a test in school? *(Allow responses.)* To take a test, you usually need a pencil *(hold up yours)* and some paper. Then you probably will go to the pencil sharpener, put the pencil in, and turn the crank. Can you imagine what the pencil feels like? *(Allow responses.)* Right! Pencils don't have feelings.

And what about the paper? When a person writes down the answers on the test paper *(hold up a sample)*, the person may push the pencil a little too hard and poke a hole right through it. See? *(Do so.)*

Well, it doesn't hurt the pencil or the paper when you use them to help you take a test.

The Bible tells us about a different kind of test. It

was a test that God gave to Abraham. God had promised a son to Abraham and Sarah. Finally little baby Isaac was born. Abraham loved Isaac more than anything else in the whole world.

God wanted to know if Abraham loved Isaac more than he loved God. So God gave Abraham a test. He commanded Abraham to take his little son, Isaac, way up in the mountains and kill him as an offering to God.

What a terribly hard test for Abraham! He had to get some wood and a knife. Because they didn't have matches to light a fire in those days, they had to take along some burning coals in a firepot.

Then they started out. At first some of Abraham's servants helped to carry the wood, but when they got near the mountain of sacrifice, the servants stayed behind.

At last they got to the place. Abraham built an altar and put the wood on it. Then came the really hard part of the test. Abraham had to tie little Isaac's hands and feet and lay him on the altar.

Just like Abraham loved his son, Isaac, so little Isaac must have loved his father, Abraham, very much too. Isaac must have believed that what his father was doing was right because the Bible doesn't say that Isaac cried or tried to hide or run away.

But Isaac must have felt like a pencil in the pencil sharpener, or like a test paper that was getting all marked up. How glad both Abraham and Isaac must have been when God said, "Stop, Abraham. Now I know you love me even more than you love your son, Isaac."

Isaac helped Abraham pass God's test. We can still help one another show our love for God. That may be hard sometimes but every time you take a test try to think of how you can help others show that they love God and ways that you can show God that you really love him too.

Esau

Concept: Choose the most important things
Objects: Pictures of good things to eat and a
Bible
Text: Mark 8:36

*What good is it for a man to gain the whole world, yet
forfeit his soul?*

Today I have some pictures I'd like to show you.
(Show some of the pictures.) The first one is of a big
strawberry pie. Doesn't it look yummy? *(Show another
picture.)* Most of us would like to have a dish of this,
or how about this? *(Show another.)* Did you know that
the hungrier you are, the better the food that you
eat seems to taste? If you are really hungry, you don't
say, "I don't like that."

Sometimes we see pictures on TV of people who
are so hungry they are almost starving to death. They
don't say they want butter and peanut butter and
jelly on their bread. No, they are happy if someone
gives them just plain bread.

Food is important; we need food to keep us alive
and to help us grow. But sometimes we think too
much about food and not enough about God.

In the Bible there is a story about a man who did

that. His name was Esau. Because Esau was the oldest son of his father, Isaac, he was to be given the birthright, a special blessing from God.

One day Esau went hunting, but he didn't find any animals he could shoot for food. When he came back he was tired and hungry. As he got close to camp, he smelled something good. His younger brother, Jacob, was making bean soup. Esau asked Jacob for some soup to eat.

Jacob wanted Esau's birthright blessing and now he thought he saw a chance to get it. So Jacob said, "First, sell me your birthright, then I'll give you the soup."

Esau had to make a choice. Was the food he was hungry for right now more important than the birthright blessing he would get much later?

Esau chose the food. But it was a bad choice. The food that would take only a few minutes to eat was not nearly as important as God's blessing that he just gave away. Esau chose the bean soup and gave up God's blessing. What a poor choice!

Sometimes we have to make choices, too. We may have to choose between different kinds of food. We may have to choose between things that are really important and those that are not so important. We often must choose between what is right and what is wrong.

When Jesus said "what good is it for a man to gain the whole world, yet forfeit his soul?" he was telling us to be very careful when we make choices.

Let's ask Jesus to help us make right choices. Let's fold our hands and pray together.

Dear Lord Jesus, It's so hard to always make right choices. We ask that you will help us to choose things that are right and good. Keep us from making choices that are foolish and wrong. In your name we pray. Amen.

Jacob

Concept: God is everywhere

Object: A stepladder

Text: Genesis 28:16

When Jacob awoke from his sleep, he thought, "Surely the LORD is in this place, and I was not aware of it."

How many of you know what this is? *(Allow responses.)* Yes, it's a ladder! Have you ever tried to climb a ladder? *(Allow responses.)* When you do, you must be very careful because if you get too high, or if the ladder is wobbly, you might fall.

Today I want to tell you a story from the Bible about a man whose name was Jacob. Jacob had a dream about a ladder.

Jacob had done a very bad thing. First he lied to his father, Isaac. Isaac was very old. He was blind and couldn't see which of his twin sons was Esau and which was Jacob. When father Isaac asked Jacob if he was Esau, his twin brother, Jacob told a lie. He said he was Esau. Jacob even put goat skins on his arms to trick his blind father.

Isaac wanted to give Esau a blessing but Jacob wanted that blessing for himself. After Isaac blessed

Jacob, Jacob had to run to a strange country far away so that Esau would not kill him.

One night, when Jacob was all by himself under the stars, he lay down to sleep. He used a stone for a pillow. While he was asleep he dreamed about a ladder, not a short one like this *(point to the stepladder)*, but a great big one that reached like a stairway all the way from earth to heaven. In his dream he saw angels going up and down the ladder.

While Jacob was asleep, he heard God speak to him and God promised all the land of that place to Jacob's children. Then he made another special promise to Jacob. God said,

"I am with you and will watch over you wherever you go."

Then Jacob woke up and thought, "Surely the LORD is in this place, and I was not aware of it."

When Jacob lay down to sleep on a lonely hillside, he thought he was alone. He thought God would never see him or keep watch over him there.

Sometimes we're just like Jacob. We think God is far away and that he isn't watching over us. But God used a ladder in a dream to remind Jacob that he really was close by.

We don't need to dream about a ladder to tell us that God is always close to us. We know that God watches over us at night too because the Bible tells us that "he never sleeps."

Whenever you see a ladder, think of Jacob's dream. Then remember that even when we aren't thinking about God, he is always near. Remember that he always watches over us and keeps us in his care just like he watched over Jacob long ago.

10

Joseph

Concept: God always has control over our lives

Object: A bright colored shirt or blouse

Text: Genesis 50:20

You intended to harm me, but God intended it for good to accomplish what is now being done, the saving of many lives.

How do you like my pretty shirt (or blouse)? *(Point to the various colors and ask, "What color is this?" or "How many different colors are there in all?")*

There is a story in the Bible about a father whose name was Jacob. Jacob had twelve sons but he loved one son, Joseph, more than the others, and so he gave Joseph a special coat—a beautiful coat of many colors.

When father Jacob gave Joseph the special coat, the other brothers started getting jealous and they began to hate Joseph. They hated Joseph so much they even planned to kill him.

Instead of killing Joseph, they sold him as a slave to some merchants who were traveling with their camels to Egypt. In Egypt Joseph had to work as a slave and was even put in prison for a while. But

God never forgot Joseph. Instead God blessed Joseph in everything he did so that the ruler of Egypt, King Pharaoh, made Joseph the next highest ruler of the whole country.

There must have been many times when Joseph wondered if God had forgotten all about him—when his brothers sold him, when he was a slave, when he was in prison, or when he was lonesome for his father and mother. But in everything that happened to Joseph, God had a plan. God used Joseph to save his people at a time of famine when there was very little food to eat.

Later, after father Jacob died, the brothers wondered if Joseph would punish them for selling him as a slave. But instead, Joseph said something very special. Joseph said, "You intended to harm me, but God intended it for good . . ." (Gen. 50:20).

Joseph knew that God was always in control of his life. He knew that God could turn the bad things into good things.

Joseph remembered this and it must have made him happy even in times of trouble. Can you remember this too? It's true; God can turn even the worst things that happen to us into something good. Every time you see a shirt, a blouse, or a coat with many colors, think of Joseph's coat and remember that God is always in control of our lives.

11

The Cupbearer
of King Pharaoh

Concept: Forgetting to do good
Object: A string tied around your finger
Text: Genesis 40:23

*The chief cupbearer, however, did not remember Joseph;
he forgot him.*

Look, girls and boys; did you notice that I have
something tied around my finger? It's a string. Why
do you suppose I would tie a string around my finger? *(Allow responses.)* Yes, I have it tied around my
finger to help me remember to _____. *(Name something you must remember to do.)*

Sometimes we forget things we need to do and so
we write them down, or sometimes we just tie a
string around our finger to remind us not to forget.

In the Book of Genesis there is a story about a man
who forgot to do something he intended to do.

That man was a cupbearer to King Pharaoh. The
king was angry with his cupbearer and his baker so
he had them both thrown into prison. While they
were there each of them had a dream.

The cupbearer dreamed about three branches of a

vine with grapes. In the dream the cupbearer squeezed the juice out of the grapes and brought it to King Pharaoh to drink. The baker dreamed about carrying three baskets of bread on his head and birds eating the bread out of the top basket.

They told the dreams to Joseph and God helped Joseph explain the meaning. In three days, the cupbearer would be taken out of prison and given his former job as cupbearer to the king. The baker would be taken out of prison in three days too, but he would be hanged.

The cupbearer thanked Joseph for telling him the meaning of the dream. Then he promised to do something good. He promised that when he was out of prison he would remember Joseph and help him get out of prison too. But when the cupbearer was out of prison, he forgot about Joseph. Not until two years later when the king had a dream did the cupbearer remember that God gave Joseph the ability to tell the meaning of dreams.

Sometimes we are just like that cupbearer. We think of good things, of kind things we could and should do for others but then before we do them, we forget. Don't be like the cupbearer. If there is something good that you should do for someone but you just haven't gotten around to do it, don't put it off. Don't forget about it. Do it as soon as you can.

12

Miriam

Concept: Loving and caring for brothers and sisters

Object: A big basket with a doll in it

Texts: Exodus 2:4, 7

His sister stood at a distance to see what would happen to him. . . . Then his sister asked Pharaoh's daughter, "Shall I go and get one of the Hebrew women to nurse the baby for you?"

Today I would like to show you my basket. It's large enough to be a picnic basket. Sometimes when we go on a picnic we put our food in it.

(Point out the type of material from which it is made.) Now look at the way the basket is made. Notice how the material is woven tightly together. One strand of the material goes under or over the next one so the basket is held tightly together.

If I fold back the blanket just a bit, you can see that I have a little doll in my basket. I put the doll in the basket because I want to tell you a Bible story about a real baby who was put into a basket. That baby's name was Moses.

The story begins like this. God's people, the Hebrews, were slaves who had to work hard in the land of Egypt. Pharaoh, the king of Egypt, became afraid that there were too many Hebrew slaves so he made a terrible law. He ordered that all baby boys born to the Hebrew slaves were to be thrown into the river to drown.

When baby Moses was born, his mother didn't do what the king said. She loved her baby too much to throw him into the river. Instead she hid him for three months, but soon he was getting too big to hide. So she made a basket. She sealed it up carefully so that no water would come into it. Then she put baby Moses in the basket and let him float on the river.

Miriam was Moses' sister. She loved her little brother, too. When the basket with baby Moses inside started to float down the river, Miriam kept watching it. Then when Pharaoh's daughter found Moses in the basket, Miriam was right there to ask if she could help. Miriam loved her brother and did all she could to help take care of him.

How many of you have younger brothers or sisters? *(Allow responses.)* If you take care of them sometimes, it's more fun when they are happy and do what you want them to do, isn't it?

How many of you have older brothers or sisters who help to take care of you sometimes? *(Allow responses.)* Are you happy, and do you do what they say when they are taking care of you? *(Allow responses.)* I hope so because they can take better care of you then.

Miriam loved her baby brother, Moses, and must have enjoyed caring for him.

Today we don't have to watch our little brothers float down the river in a basket like Miriam did, but loving our brothers and sisters and helping to care for them is part of God's plan for our families too. Let's all try to be nice to our brothers and sisters just like God wants us to be.

13

Moses

Concept: Anger can lead to trouble
Object: A large piece of red cloth
Text: Numbers 20:10b–11a

"Listen, you rebels, must we bring you water out of this rock?" Then Moses raised his arm and struck the rock twice.

If I were a bullfighter and I waved my red flag like this to tease a bull, what would the bull do? *(Allow responses.)* Yes, the bull would put his big head down, point his sharp horns at the red cloth, and come charging right at it, because he gets angry when he sees the color red.

Then the bullfighter would pull the cloth away. *(Act like you were the bullfighter and pull the cloth aside.)* He would probably do this several times until the bull was really angry. But getting angry in this way will get the bull in trouble because soon the bullfighter will spear him and since the bull is so angry, he will run right back and get speared again.

Getting angry can get people into trouble too.

Long ago when Moses was leading the Israelites out of the land of Egypt into the Promised Land, they often complained because there was no water in the wilderness. One time God told Moses to speak to a rock and water for the people to drink would come out of it.

But Moses was angry with the people because they were always complaining and his anger got him into trouble. Instead of speaking to the rock like God told him to do, he took his staff and struck the rock.

God still did a miracle and made water come out of the rock for the people, but because Moses disobeyed God, he could not enter the Promised Land. Moses' anger at the people made him forget to obey God.

Did you know that anger can still get people into trouble today? If you get angry at someone, watch out! You may do something foolish like a bull does when he gets angry at a red cloth and runs into the bullfighter's spear; or you may do something wrong like Moses did when he struck the rock instead of simply speaking to it.

Best of all, don't get angry in the first place.

14

Aaron

Concept: God desires and is pleased with the prayers of his children

Objects: Various kinds of perfume, a rose or another flower

Text: Psalm 141:2

May my prayer be set before you like incense; may the lifting up of my hands be like the evening sacrifice.

Today I brought something very special. *(Show the bottles of perfume.)* It comes in little bottles of different sizes and shapes. From the outside the liquid in the bottles looks almost the same. Some of the bottles are a little different color but most look very much alike. Does anyone know what I have in these bottles? *(Allow responses.)* Yes, it is perfume. Do you know how you can tell that it's perfume and not just water? *(Allow responses.)*

The reason it smells good is because it's made out of something that smells good like this rose. *(Show girls and boys the flower and allow some of them to smell it.)* Some perfume is made from the petals of roses. A tiny bit of oil is taken out of the flower petal and put in a perfume bottle. Then the perfume smells just like the flower.

Long ago God's people would go to their church, the tabernacle. Aaron, the high priest, wore a very special robe. He would burn sweet smelling incense before the Lord on a special altar. Then Aaron would offer the incense to God. The burning incense must have smelled a lot like the perfume we have in these bottles. It must have made the whole tabernacle smell very nice. God was pleased with the offerings of sweet smelling incense that the people brought to honor and thank him.

Today we don't have to bring sweet smelling perfume to church as an offering to God. The deacons would really be surprised if somebody put a bottle of perfume in the offering plate as a gift for God.

But there is something you can do that pleases God today as much as the sweet smelling offerings that God's people brought long ago. Do you know what that is? You can bring your prayers to God.

The Bible tells us in Psalm 141:2, "May my prayer be set before you like incense." God is as pleased with our prayers today as he was when the people brought an offering of incense long ago for Aaron the high priest to burn on the altar for a sweet smell before the Lord.

Aaron had to burn the sweet smelling incense on the altar every morning when he tended the lamps, and he had to burn more incense in the evening. If our prayers are like sweet smelling incense before the Lord we must remember to pray in the morning and in the evening too.

Before you go back to your seats, I would like to put just a little perfume on your hand so you can smell it. Then, when you pray, think of the sweet smell that perfume makes, and try to remember that God is pleased when we pray.

15

Joshua

Concept: Christian families
Object: A clock
Text: Joshua 24:15c

But as for me and my household, we will serve the LORD.

Who knows what the long hand on this clock does? *(Allow responses.)* And what does the little hand show? *(Allow responses.)* Do you know how many hours there are in a day? *(Allow responses.)* Yes, there are twenty-four hours in a day. Twelve o'clock comes at noon and twelve o'clock comes at midnight.

Today I would like to tell you about a man who led the people of Israel into the Promised Land. That man's name was Joshua. Let's say that all together: *Joshua.*

One of the first enemy cities that Joshua and his armies had to fight was the city of Jericho. In Joshua chapter 6, the Bible tells the story of how Joshua's armies marched around the city and God made the walls of the city come tumbling down.

But later, as Joshua and the army of Israel moved ahead to capture the land like God told them to do, they met a very strong army of the enemy. The battle would take a long time.

Then Joshua prayed to God. He asked God for a longer day to finish the battle. Joshua asked God to make both the sun and the moon stop in their places in the sky.

God listened to Joshua's prayer. He did make the sun stop in the middle of the sky and it didn't go down for almost another whole day! Nothing like that had ever happened before and nothing like that has happened since.

Clocks *(hold up the clock)* can measure time but only God can make the time happen.

When Joshua was old he remembered how God had helped him and Israel's army win battles. He remembered how the walls of Jericho came tumbling down. He remembered how God made the sun stand still and he told his children about how great God is.

Then he asked the people whom they were going to serve. He asked them to choose to serve God. He told them what his family was going to do. He said, "But as for me and my house, we will serve the LORD."

Wasn't that great! Joshua and his whole family were going to serve the Lord together!

You're part of your family, aren't you? So you can help your family serve the Lord just like Joshua's children helped his family serve God.

When you look at the clock, try to remember that only God can make time go by; he holds the sun in the sky and makes it travel on its journey. He is a great God and you and your family can always serve him just like Joshua's family did.

16

Caleb

Concept: Believing God's promises

Objects: Bunch of grapes and a yardstick, a dowel, or other stick about 3 feet long

Text: Numbers 13:23b

They cut off a branch bearing a single cluster of grapes. Two of them carried it on a pole between them.

Do you see this bunch of grapes, boys and girls? It was the biggest bunch I could find in the grocery store. Today, I would like to tell you about a really big bunch of grapes.

In the Bible we read about the people of Israel. They had been slaves for 400 years in the land of Egypt. Then God sent ten terrible plagues and at last King Pharaoh let the people go.

Moses was their leader and God sent a pillar of cloud by day and a pillar of fire by night to lead the people to the Promised Land. They traveled through the Red Sea and across the desert.

Finally they got to the border of the land that God had promised to them. It was a rich and wonderful land, but wicked people who had strong armies lived there in cities with high walls. Some of these people were even giants.

Moses sent twelve spies into the land to find out more about it. The twelve spies looked at the beautiful land and, to show the people of Israel how fruitful it was, they cut down a bunch of grapes that was so big they had to put it on a pole. Two grown men had to carry it between them to keep it from dragging on the ground.

I have a stick here. Shall we see if two of you can carry this bunch of grapes? *(Put the yardstick or dowel through your bunch of grapes and get two boys to hold it between them on their shoulders.)* It doesn't quite touch the ground, does it? Can you imagine how big the bunch of grapes was that Caleb brought back from the Promised Land? Two grown men had to carry it on a pole between them! *(Ask boys to put down the stick and grapes before going on with the story.)*

You would think that the people of Israel would have been anxious to go to that wonderful Promised Land. But they became afraid when the spies told about the giants and the walled cities.

God had cared for the people of Israel in the desert. He had given them manna and quail to eat and water to drink. God had even kept their shoes from wearing out! But they forgot how great God is! They didn't believe God's promises. Only two of the twelve spies, Joshua and Caleb, believed that God could protect them and would bring them safely into the Promised Land. Joshua later became the leader of Israel. God gave a special promise to Caleb, too. All the other people of Israel over twenty years old would die in the desert. But because Joshua and

Caleb believed God's promises and trusted in him, they were able to go into the Promised Land.

Many years later, when Caleb settled on the land given to him, he must have had a vineyard of grapes. Maybe they were great big clusters so that he needed the help of his children to pick them.

Every time Caleb picked grapes, he must have been reminded of God's promises. Caleb believed God's promises and he entered the Promised Land.

God has promised that one day we will be with him in heaven. Heaven is our Promised Land. We need to trust Jesus to bring us there just like Caleb needed to trust God to bring him into the Promised Land long ago.

Every time you see a bunch of grapes, think of how good and great God is. Let the grapes remind you of God's promises about heaven and then place your trust in him.

17

Achan

Concept: Coveting can lead to other sins

Objects: A collection of gold or silver jewelry on a tray

Text: Joshua 7:21

When I saw . . . a beautiful robe . . . , two hundred shekels of silver and a wedge of gold . . . , I coveted them and took them.

All of these things, the watches, chains, and other jewelry, are made of either gold or silver, girls and boys. Gold and silver are called precious metals because they are quite hard to find. Today mining companies use special machinery to dig these metals out of the earth. Long ago miners had to dig up the silver and pan out the gold by hand. It was hard work and very little of the metal was found. People who had some silver or gold were thought to be very rich.

Long ago, when Joshua and the people of Israel fought against the city of Jericho, God made the walls tumble down and Israel won the battle. Joshua told the soldiers of Israel to burn what was left of the city, but before they did that they were to take all the gold and silver and save it for the treasury of the Lord to be used later when they built the temple.

But one soldier whose name was Achan didn't do what Joshua told him to do. Achan saw a nice robe and instead of destroying it, he wanted it for himself. Then he saw some silver and some gold and he wanted that too. First he wanted it, and then he took it. He dug a hole in the floor of his tent, and there he hid the things that he had taken. He thought no one would know what he had done.

Achan forgot that God sees everything we do. God saw Achan take the things that he should not have taken. God saw Achan dig a hole and hide the things he had stolen.

The next day the army of Israel went to fight a small city by the name of Ai. Israel lost the battle because God was displeased with Achan's sin. All Israel had to stand before the Lord so the guilty person could be found.

First the tribe of Judah was taken. Then the clan of the Zerahites was taken, then the family of Zimri was taken, and finally this family had to come forward man by man until Achan was taken. God knew who had stolen the silver and gold. Achan and all his family were stoned and burned. What a terrible punishment for stealing things that did not belong to him!

Achan first saw the silver and gold, then he wanted it, and next he took it. He thought they were more important than obeying God.

When you see silver and gold like this, girls and boys *(show the tray again)*, remember that they are just metals that miners dig out of the earth. The metals are heated to make them pure and then the metals are made into all different kinds of things.

But no metal is more important than doing what God wants us to do. We have to love God most of all, more than all the silver and gold in the whole world! Be sure to remember that. Don't make the mistake that Achan made!

18

Gideon

Concept: Searching for God's will in our lives
Object: A fleece of sheepskin
Text: Judges 6:37

I will place a wool fleece on the threshing floor. If there is dew only on the fleece and all the ground is dry, then I will know that you will save Israel by my hand, as you said.

Do you know what this is? *(Show the piece of wool sheepskin. Allow responses.)* Yes, it's sheepskin, and it feels woolly and warm. *(Allow children to touch it.)*

Today I would like to tell you a Bible story about a man named Gideon. Gideon lived at a time when the enemies of God's people, Israel, would come and steal their crops and animals.

You see, Israel had started to worship idols and other false gods, instead of the one true God. Then God came to Gideon and told him to destroy the false gods and fight against the enemies of Israel.

But the armies of the enemy were so large and the army of Gideon was so small. Gideon was afraid. He wanted to know if God would really be with him in the battle, so Gideon asked God for a sign.

Gideon would lay the fleece of wool on the ground outside at night, and if the fleece was wet with dew and all the ground around it was dry, Gideon would know that God would give him the victory.

You know that when the grass is wet with dew in the morning, all the grass gets wet. It would be a miracle if one spot was dry and all the rest was wet. Gideon knew that only God could make the fleece wet and leave the ground around it dry.

But God did what Gideon asked. One night God made the fleece wet and the ground dry and the next night he made the fleece dry and the ground around it wet with dew. Then Gideon knew that if God could do this miracle, God could surely help him win the battle too.

That was a nice way for Gideon to be sure that he would do what God wanted him to do, wasn't it? Sometimes we have trouble deciding things. That's true of boys and girls, but it will be true when you grow up too.

You may have to make an important decision and you wish God would just tell you what to do. You may wish that you could lay a fleece like this *(hold it up)* out on the lawn and if it was wet the answer would be "Yes," or if it was dry the answer would be "No."

But today God wants us to pray to him instead. If we have a problem or question, it doesn't matter if it's large or small; we can take our problems and questions to Jesus in prayer and he will help us find the answer.

51

So the next time you have to make an important choice in your life, remember the time when Gideon wanted to be sure that he was doing what God wanted him to do. Remember to pray to God for wisdom. Ask Jesus to help you make the right choices in your life.

19

Samson

Concept: For real strength you must depend on God

Object: A few riddles

Text: Judges 14:14

Out of the eater, something to eat;
out of the strong, something sweet.

Girls and boys, how many of you like riddles? *(Allow responses.)* Today I would like to see how good you are at answering some riddles. Here's the first one: What has four legs but cannot walk? *(Allow responses.)* Good! Here's another one: What three words do pupils use most in school? *(Allow responses. "I don't know" is the correct answer.)* Right! Let's just try one more; they're getting harder: When you play ball, does it take longer to run from first base to second, or from second base to third? *(Allow responses.* The answer is: From second to third because there's a short stop in the middle.)

Riddles are fun; I like them too. Did you know that there is a riddle in the Bible?

The man who asked the riddle was Samson. Samson was a judge, a leader of God's people, Israel. God made Samson so strong that he could carry the gates of a city on his shoulders. When a lion tried to kill him, Samson killed the lion instead. Later when Samson went by that same place again he saw some bees had gathered honey and were storing it in the dead lion's body. He took some of the honey and gave some to his parents too.

Then he made up this riddle:

"Out of the eater, something to eat;
Out of the strong, something sweet."

When Samson was going to get married to a Philistine woman, he asked his riddle of those at the wedding feast. They couldn't guess the answer so they forced Samson's new wife to get the answer from Samson. When he told her the answer, she told it to her people, the Philistines. The answer was:

"What is sweeter than honey?
What is stronger than a lion?"

Later in Samson's life, when the Philistines were trying to kill him, they tied him with new ropes, and even wove his long hair in a weaver's beam. God gave Samson so much strength that he was always able to get away from them.

Delilah, Samson's Philistine wife, kept asking him what made him so strong. Finally Samson told her that he was a special servant of the God of Israel. In those days, if a person was a Nazarite, a special servant of God, he could never cut his hair. If Delilah would shave off his hair he would be no stronger than anyone else.

After Samson fell asleep, what do you think Delilah did? Yes, she cut off his hair and called the Philistines. They made him a slave and took out his eyes. Samson was not faithful to God so God left him. At the very end of his life, Samson prayed to God and asked God to give him strength once more.

And what do you think God did? *(Allow responses.)* Yes, God heard Samson's prayer, just like he hears all of our prayers. That's how great and how good God is!

20

Ruth

Concept: Choose to be with God's people

Objects: Church bulletin and entertainment page from local newspaper

Text: Ruth 1:16b

Where you go I will go, and where you stay I will stay. Your people will be my people and your God my God.

Do you see how many different kinds of things are going on in our community today? *(Show the entertainment page from the local newspaper.)* There are _____ *(mention a few things they could have attended instead of going to church). (Next, show the church bulletin.)* But there's another important thing going on too, and that's the worship service in our church.

I'm glad you chose to be here with God's people. That was the right choice and it was a very important choice to make. Today there are so many other things to do that it is sometimes hard to choose to be with God's people to worship God in church.

The Bible tells us about a young woman named Ruth from the land of Moab. She had married Naomi's son but he died. Then Naomi decided to go back to the land of Israel, back to her people in the little town of Bethlehem. She told Ruth to stay in the land of Moab.

But Ruth had learned about the true God, the God of Israel and she wanted to be with God's people. She said to Naomi,

"Where you go I will go, and where you stay I will stay. Your people will be my people and your God my God."

Ruth made an important choice. She chose to be with God's people. Because of this important choice, God blessed Ruth. He gave her a new husband, Boaz, and she became the great-grandmother of King David. She lived in Bethlehem, the place where Jesus was born, of the house and lineage of David.

Ruth's choice to be with God's people gave her a part in bringing the Savior into the world. That choice was a blessing to Ruth *and* to all the rest of God's people.

When you need to choose between being with God's people or being with those who do not love or care about God, remember Ruth's choice.

If you choose to be with God's people you will receive a blessing from them and they will be blessed because you are with them. The next time you wonder whether or not you should go to church, think of Ruth and remember how important it is to choose to be with God's people.

21

Samuel

Concept: Listening to God
Object: Radio or tape recorder with ear
 phones
Text: 1 Samuel 3:9b

Speak, LORD, for your servant is listening.

How many of you have ever had ear phones on
your ears? *(Show the ear phones to the children; try them
on or allow a child to do so.)* Why do people wear ear
phones? *(Allow responses.)*

Yes, ear phones can help you to listen more carefully, and they can help you to listen to just what
you want to hear without bothering or being both-
ered by others.

Listening is not always easy to do, is it? Sometimes
our mothers ask us to do something and we are so
busy playing or doing something else that we just
don't hear them.

Or, if you're in church school class and the teacher
is telling a Bible story and you start thinking about
something else, you just forget to listen and you
can't remember what the story was about. Did you
know that this even happens to older people in
church sometimes while the minister is preaching?

Our minds can start thinking about something else and we just forget to listen.

The Bible tells us about a little boy named Samuel. Samuel was a very special little boy because his mother, Hannah, promised God that she would take Samuel to live in the temple when he was old enough to be away from home. Each year his mother made a little robe and brought it to the temple at Jerusalem for Samuel.

Samuel helped Eli the high priest care for the temple lamps and keep the temple clean. Samuel even slept in the temple.

One night God called to Samuel. He said, "Samuel, Samuel." At first Samuel thought it was Eli calling him and he hurried to Eli to see what he could do for him. But Eli had not called for Samuel. When God called the third time, Eli knew it was God who was calling Samuel and he told Samuel to say, "Speak, Lord, for your servant is listening."

Wasn't that a wonderful thing to say? "Yes, God, I'm listening!"

We hear God's Word in church; we hear God's Word every time we read the Bible. It's so easy to forget to listen, or to think about something else so we just don't hear what God is saying to us.

When Jesus was teaching the people who followed him, he must have noticed that some people weren't listening because he said, "He who has ears to hear, let him hear."

God gave us ears to hear his Word. We can enjoy using ear phones like this *(hold up those you have)* for listening to music.

But it's more important to do what Samuel did. He listened when God spoke to him. When we hear God's Word let's try to be good listeners too.

22

King Saul

Concept: God honors those who are humble

Object: Game of "Pin the Tail on the Donkey"

Text: 1 Samuel 10:22–24

Today I'd like to show you a game that some of you may know about—it's called "Pin the Tail on the Donkey." Look at the picture of a donkey over here *(draw attention to picture)*—notice that its tail is lost. Also, I have a tail and a blindfold. To play the game we need to blindfold someone *(select a volunteer)* and ask that person to pin a tail on the donkey. Let's choose _____ to try. *(After one child has had a turn, select one more.)* Both of you did very well, and we're glad the donkey has his lost tail back.

Now I'd like to tell you about some other donkeys. They didn't just lose their tails, they all got lost.

The donkeys belonged to a man in the Bible by the name of Kish. We don't know how they got lost. Maybe the people who were supposed to tie them up forgot to do so, or maybe they just wandered away.

Well, Kish wanted his donkeys back so he sent his son, Saul, out to hunt for them.

Saul and some servants looked for many days. They kept looking for so long that they went quite far away. Saul was gone so long that father Kish stopped worrying about his donkeys and started worrying about his son, Saul.

But God knew where Saul was. God sent his prophet, Elisha, to tell Saul that the donkeys had been found. God also told Elisha to anoint Saul to be king over his people Israel.

The new King Saul was big and tall—so tall that the rest of the people were only as high as Saul's shoulders. But when the people came to make him king, they couldn't find him. Saul was hiding in the baggage!

That means that Saul was not proud of being chosen to be king. He didn't want everybody to look at him and say how important he was. Instead he was humble because he knew that God was the real king of his people Israel.

As long as King Saul was humble and depended on God for all his needs, God blessed Saul in all his battles. But then something very sad happened. King Saul started to become proud. He began to think he didn't need God anymore.

When Saul forgot about God, God stopped blessing Saul. Instead of winning the battles, Saul and his armies would lose them. The life of King Saul came to a very sad ending because he became proud and thought he didn't need God anymore.

Too bad he didn't stay humble the way he was when he first became king.

Whenever you see a picture of a donkey, or play a game of "Pin the Tail on the Donkey," or even if you see a real donkey, think about King Saul who hunted for his father's donkeys. And then remember not to be proud but to be humble the way Saul was when he first became King of Israel.

23

David

Concept: Defending the honor of God's people

Objects: Five small stones and a sling(shot)

Text: 1 Samuel 17:45

David said to the Philistine, "You come against me with sword and spear and javelin, but I come against you in the name of the LORD Almighty, the God of the armies of Israel, whom you have defied."

Do any of you know what I have here in my hands? *(Show the class the slingshot and the five stones. Allow responses.)* You're right. If I pull the slingshot back like this, put a stone in it, and let it go, it would probably make the stone fly right through one of the church windows over there. We wouldn't want that to happen, so I'll just keep it here by me.

Today I would like to tell you about a man in the Bible who knew how to use a slingshot (or sling) very well. That man was David. When David was a boy he had to take care of his father's sheep.

The sling that David had was probably only made of a cord with a part in it that would hold a stone. Sometimes wild animals would try to kill the sheep and David would chase them away with his sling.

Then he would swing it around and around and at just the right time he would let the stone fly out to hit what he was aiming at.

One day David went to visit his older brothers in the army. The army of God's people, Israel, was fighting against the army of the Philistines and at that time David saw the huge Philistine soldier named Goliath.

Goliath would laugh at the army of God's people and would say bad things about them. Because Goliath was so big and strong the soldiers of Israel were afraid and would not go to fight him.

But David wasn't afraid. He knew God would be with him. Then using his sling and a few stones, he went out to fight Goliath. David said to Goliath, "I come against you in the name of the Lord Almighty, the God of the armies of Israel, whom you have defied." And God helped David win the battle!

The Bible says that Goliath "defied" the people of Israel—God's people. That means that he made fun of them and laughed at them.

Did you know that God's people still get laughed at today? Yes, they do! People who don't love Jesus still like to make fun of Christians.

What are Christians supposed to do if others make fun of them? Should they throw stones at them and fight them? When Jesus came to earth he gave us a better way.

Instead of fighting our enemies, Jesus told us to love them. Jesus said: "If your enemy is hungry, feed him; if he is thirsty, give him something to drink."

It's hard to love your enemies, isn't it? But when we are angry and feel more like throwing stones, we need to drop the stones and love our enemies instead. That's what Jesus wants us to do. Let's all try to do that.

24

Solomon

Concept: Learning helpful proverbs
Objects: An ant farm, flat lid, and sugar
Text: Proverbs 6:6

Go to the ant, you sluggard;
consider its ways and be wise!

This is my ant farm; see how busy the ants are. How many of you have ever seen little ants running along on the sidewalk? *(Allow responses.)* Did you ever notice that they always seem to be hurrying to go someplace? Some of them may be carrying heavy loads of things to eat. They carry the food back to their home.

If you like to watch ants, you might like to try this: get a flat lid something like this one *(show the one you have),* and lay it on the ground near where you think some ants may live. Put a little sugar on the lid—you may even want to spill a little on the ground around it. After a short time one ant will find it and that one ant will tell others. Soon there will be lots of ants that want to taste the sugar, and, because ants are very wise, they may even carry the sugar back to their home to save it and eat it later, maybe in the winter when the weather is cold.

But now let me tell you a short story from the Bible about the wisest man who ever lived. His name was King Solomon.

When Solomon first became king, God came to him in a dream and told Solomon that he could ask for anything he wanted and God would give it to him. Wouldn't it be nice to have a dream like that? If you or I had a dream like that, I wonder what we would ask for?

Well, Solomon knew he would have to be very wise to be a good king over God's people so he asked God to give him wisdom so that he could be a wise ruler.

God gave Solomon what he asked for. God made King Solomon the wisest man who ever lived. People like the Queen of Sheba came from far away to ask him questions and listen to his answers.

One thing that King Solomon did was to write many wise sayings. A wise saying is called a proverb and many of Solomon's proverbs are in the Bible in the Book of Proverbs. We can still learn a great deal from them. Some of the proverbs are written for young people and some for old people. One of Solomon's wise sayings was written for lazy people.

This is what Solomon wrote: "Go to the ant, you sluggard [that's a lazy person]; consider its ways and be wise."

That proverb tells lazy people to go and look at the ants. Watch them hurry as they work hard to gather food and save it for winter; they aren't lazy at all.

We can't be as wise as King Solomon. But we can read many of his wise sayings in the Bible. The Book of Proverbs in the Bible is right after Psalms so it is real easy to find.

But just reading them or listening to others read them to us isn't enough. Even learning them by heart isn't enough. We have to try to do what they say if we want to be really wise.

25

Elijah

Concept: Our strength to face trouble comes from God

Objects: A pan of snow or sand and water

Text: 1 Kings 19:4b

He [Elijah] came to a broom tree, sat down under it and prayed that he might die. "I have had enough, LORD," he said. "Take my life; I am no better than my ancestors."

It really is fun to build a snowman (or a sand castle), isn't it? *(As you build a miniature snowman or a small sand castle, describe to the girls and boys what you are doing and even allow them to assist you if possible.)* Have any of you tried to do this? *(Allow responses.)*

You can do all kinds of things to make them look real. But after the weather gets warm, what gradually happens to the snowman? (Or, after the tide comes in and the wind blows, what happens to the sand castle?)

Yes, the snowman melts and gradually disappears (or the sand castle gradually just sinks away) and then it is gone. The place where it was standing looks like it was never there at all. It isn't long and even the person who built it forgets it.

Well, did you know that sometimes when trouble comes, people would like to be something like a snowman (or sand castle)? The trouble seems so strong that they would just like to melt (or fade) away and disappear.

Let me tell you about one of God's great prophets who once felt that way. His name was Elijah. At the time that Elijah lived, the very wicked King Ahab and his wicked wife Jezebel were ruling Israel.

Because Israel did not worship God, he kept the rain from falling for three years. Then God's prophet, Elijah, told the prophets of the false god, Baal, to meet him on the top of Mt. Carmel.

There Elijah built an altar to the true God and the prophets of Baal built an altar to their false god, Baal. They agreed that the god who would send fire from heaven to the altar would be the true God. Only the true God, Elijah's God, could do this. Then they killed the false prophets of Baal and God sent rain on the thirsty land. After that the wicked Queen Jezebel said she was going to kill Elijah. Then Elijah became afraid. He ran away into the desert and sat under a tree, wishing that he could die. He thought the trouble was so big that he just wished he could be like a snowman (or sand castle) and fade away.

But then God came to Elijah. God knew what Elijah needed to give him courage again. God gave Elijah food to strengthen his body. He appeared to Elijah in a still, small voice to give him courage, and then God gave Elijah some jobs to do. Well, that's just what Elijah needed. Elijah went to work for God again.

What must you do if trouble comes? Don't just wish you were a snowman (or a sand castle) and wish you could fade away. No, do what Elijah did. First pray to God. Then look for something that God would want you to do and go to work for him.

26

Elisha

Concept: God is all-powerful and everywhere

Objects: A pan of water, objects that float—a piece of wood and a plastic toy, and objects that sink—a nail, and an axe head

Text: 2 Kings 6:6b, 16

Elisha cut a stick and threw it there, and made the iron float.

"Don't be afraid," the prophet answered. "Those who are with us are more than those who are with them."

I have a pan of water I would like to use in our Bible lesson, girls and boys. First I would like to show you this piece of wood. If I place the wood on the water, do you think it will sink or float? *(Allow responses.)* OK, let's try. . . . Right, the wood floats. Next I'll try this nail. What do you think will happen now? *(Allow responses.)* Well, let's see if it will sink or float. *(Drop it in the water.)* Right, it went right to the bottom. Now let's try this plastic toy. What do you think will happen now? *(Allow responses.)* Right, now I have one more item to try. This is the head of an axe. What do you suppose will happen to this? *(Allow responses.)* Well, let's try. Yes, it went right to the bottom because it is so heavy.

In the Bible there is a story about an axe head that floated. It happened during the time of the prophet Elisha. As a group of prophets who were with Elisha were cutting down trees, the head of the axe used by one of the young men came off and fell into the Jordan River. The young man was really worried because he had borrowed the axe. Then he brought the problem to Elisha who was a prophet of God. God used Elisha to do a miracle. He made the axe head float like a piece of wood or a plastic toy. The young prophet could just reach out and take it.

A little later, the enemies of God's people came with horses and chariots and surrounded the city where Elisha was. Elisha's servant was afraid and he cried out, "Oh, my lord, what shall we do?" Then Elisha prayed that God would open the eyes of his servant so he could see all of God's army that was around them to protect them.

Whenever we are afraid, we have to remember how great God is. Long ago when one of the prophets was in trouble, God did a miracle to make the axe head float. When they were in danger God surrounded his servants with unseen armies to protect them. God is still as powerful and wonderful today as he was then. God always gives us what is best for us and he has promised in the Bible that he will send his angels to watch over us. We really don't have to be afraid. Let's try to remember that our powerful, loving God is always near to care for us and protect us wherever we are.

27

Naaman's Servant Girl

Concept: Every Christian has an important
    mission
Object: A jigsaw puzzle
Text: 2 Kings 5:3

*She said to her mistress, "If only my master would see
the prophet who is in Samaria! He would cure him of his
leprosy."*

Today I brought a jigsaw puzzle, girls and boys.
*(Show the box of a rather simple jigsaw puzzle with large
pieces. Have three sides of the outside edge already assem-
bled on a flat board that you can tip up a bit so children
see the puzzle.)* Look at the picture on the box. *(Com-
ment on the picture the puzzle will make.)* What do you
have to do to make the puzzle look like the picture?
(Allow responses.) Right! One of the best ways to start
is to pick out four pieces that look like corners. *(Point
out the four corner pieces.)* Next find all the pieces that
have a flat side and put them together to make the
edge. *(Point to edge you have partially completed and fit
in last few pieces to complete the outside edge of the puzzle.)* Then the rest seems to be easy to put together.
(Keep one large and important piece in your pocket.) Oh,
oh, it looks like one of the pieces of my puzzle is

missing. Did you ever put a puzzle together and find that a piece was missing? When pieces are missing, puzzles don't turn out nice.

Life is something like a jigsaw puzzle. All the parts need to fit together to make the picture complete. I would like to tell you a Bible story with lots of parts.

One part was an army commander named Naaman who had a bad disease called leprosy. Another part was all the false gods of the country where Naaman lived. They were not really God at all so they couldn't heal Naaman's leprosy.

Another part of the puzzle was the people of Samaria who knew about the true God, the God of Israel. Then there was Elisha, a prophet of God who lived in Samaria.

Naaman needed to know about God. Elisha knew about God. Just like two pieces of the puzzle. But they needed one other little piece to hook them together.

Naaman's wife had a little servant girl. The Bible doesn't even tell us her name. She was the missing piece. She connected Naaman who needed God with Elisha who knew God.

The little servant girl told Naaman's wife about Elisha, the prophet of the true God, the God of Israel. She said that if Naaman would go to see Elisha, God could heal his leprosy.

Naaman's wife told Naaman. Naaman went to see Elisha. God told Elisha to tell Naaman to wash in the Jordan River seven times. Then God did a wonderful miracle. He healed Naaman's leprosy.

It never would have happened if the little servant girl had been too afraid or too ashamed to tell someone else about God. She was the part of the puzzle that made it complete.

If you know about God, you're something like that little servant girl. If there are other people who don't go to church and don't love Jesus, they are something like Naaman.

How can people who don't know about God get hooked up to God? All of us Christians will just have to try to hook them together just like this missing piece in the puzzle. *(Take the last piece out of your pocket and finish the puzzle.)*

28

Nehemiah

Concept: Happiness shows on your face
Objects: Pictures of sad and smiling faces
Text: Nehemiah 2:2

Why does your face look so sad when you are not ill? This can be nothing but sadness of heart.

Look at this big smiling face, boys and girls. Do you think that this is a happy face? *(Allow responses.)* Why do you think this is a happy face? *(Allow responses.)* Now look at this face. *(Show picture of face with a frown and perhaps some teardrops.)* Do you think this is a happy face? *(Allow responses.)*

Right! And the reason a person smiles and laughs or frowns and cries is because of the way the person feels inside. You hardly ever cry if you feel happy inside, and you hardly ever laugh or smile if you feel sad inside.

You can tell if a person is happy or sad just by looking at the face of that person. People who lived long ago could do this too.

The Bible tells us about Nehemiah, a young man who lived many, many hundreds of years ago, long before Jesus was born. Nehemiah had a very special

78

job. He was a cupbearer who brought wine to the king. He was always happy when he did this.

But then one day Nehemiah heard some sad news. He learned that Jerusalem, the city where King David had lived when he was ruler of Israel and the city where King Solomon had built a beautiful temple to God, was all destroyed. Enemies had come to knock down the walls and burn the gates with fire.

Nehemiah was sad because he heard bad news about the city of God and God's temple. And the sadness in his heart showed on his face. It showed so much that the king noticed Nehemiah's sadness.

The king asked Nehemiah what was making him sad. Then Nehemiah told the king that Jerusalem, the city of his homeland and the place where his fathers were buried was destroyed. The king was kind to Nehemiah and gave him permission to go and rebuild Jerusalem. The king even gave Nehemiah letters so that he could get lumber and other supplies that he would need.

Rebuilding Jerusalem was hard work and many enemies tried to stop Nehemiah but finally it was finished. The smile must have come back to Nehemiah's face because we read in Nehemiah eight, verse ten, that he said, "Do not grieve, for the joy of the LORD is your strength."

Nehemiah was sad when the city and temple of God were in trouble; he was happy when the things of God were going well.

If somebody destroyed your church or told you that you couldn't go to church today, would you be sad like Nehemiah was when he learned that Jerusalem was destroyed? Would your face look like this? *(Hold up sad face.)*

Or are you happy to be in church today like Nehemiah was when Jerusalem and the temple were rebuilt? Then your face should look like this. *(Hold up smiling face.)* Let's try to keep the smiles on to show that we're happy to be here today.

29

Haman

Concept: Pride is like a soap bubble that bursts

Object: Soap bubble equipment

Texts: Esther 6:6b; 7:10

Now Haman thought to himself, "Who is there that the king would rather honor than me?". . . So they hanged Haman on the gallows he had prepared for Mordecai.

I like to make soap bubbles, don't you? Just put the bubble maker in the soapy liquid like this, hold it up, and blow softly. *(Do so.)* There come the bubbles. Or you can dip it in and just slowly swing your arm through the air and there come some more pretty bubbles.

How long do you think it will be before the bubbles pop?

Look at this one. *(Make another.)* Let's see how long it will be before it bursts. Oh, oh, there it goes; it's all gone. Soap bubbles are really pretty while they last, but they don't last long.

Sometimes when people feel proud of who they are and what they do, their feeling of how important they are bursts just like a soap bubble.

There is a story in the Bible, in the Book of Esther,

about a man who thought he was really important. His name was Haman. The king often asked Haman's advice. The king even gave Haman the ring used to seal new laws for the kingdom.

Haman was so proud he wanted everyone to bow down to him when he rode along the street on his horse. But one man by the name of Mordecai wouldn't bow down to Haman. Because Mordecai was a Jew he would bow down only to the God of Israel. This made Haman so angry, he decided to have Mordecai killed. He had his servants build a huge gallows 75 feet high to hang Mordecai on.

Then Queen Esther invited the king and Haman to a banquet. That made Haman feel even more important. His life was like a beautiful big soap bubble. He was so proud.

But then the trouble started for Haman. The king couldn't sleep one night and he had his servants read the records of the kingdom to him. The king learned that at one time Mordecai, the Jew, had saved his life. To honor Mordecai, the king ordered Haman to put the king's robe on Mordecai and let Mordecai ride the king's horse. Haman had to lead the horse and Mordecai got to ride. How humiliating for proud Haman!

But worse things were to come. When the king and Haman came to Queen Esther's banquet, the queen told the king that Haman had a plan to kill all the Jews. The king became very angry at Haman and ordered that Haman should be hung on the very gallows he had built to hang Mordecai on.

Haman was very proud. For a while his life was like a pretty soap bubble. But it was as empty inside as a soap bubble is. He was floating along thinking only of himself when suddenly the bubble burst. Haman's life ended like a soap bubble bursting. Nothing was left.

What can we learn from this Bible story? One thing is that we should remember to think of others and not just ourselves. Instead of wanting others to praise us, we should remember to praise God. Let's try to do that. Then our lives won't be like empty soap bubbles that just look pretty for a few seconds and then burst. Instead, our lives will be filled with real and lasting beauty as we live for Jesus.

Job

Concept: God may choose to send us bad as well as good things

Object: Newspaper headlines (a few that show bad things and a few that show good things)

Text: Job 2:10b

Shall we accept good from God, and not trouble?

Isn't this good news? *(Read.)* **LOST CHILD IS FOUND** or **GOOD WHEAT HARVEST IS EXPECTED** or . . . *(use a "good news" headline you have found).*

It's nice to get good news, isn't it? But all news isn't good.

Look at a few more of these headlines . . . **PLANE CRASHES AND ALL ABOARD ARE LOST** or **NUMBER OF HOMELESS PEOPLE IS GROWING** or . . . *(use a few "bad news" headlines you have found).*

Do you sometimes listen to the news on the radio or watch it on TV? *(Allow responses.)* Maybe you noticed that sometimes the news is good. Then it makes you feel happy. But sometimes the news is bad because it tells about bad things that happen to people.

The Bible tells us about a man who lived long ago.

His name was Job. When the story began, Job was very rich. God had given Job many sheep and oxen. He owned camels and donkeys and had many servants. He had seven sons and three daughters and he worshiped God every day. Everything seemed to be going very well. Life for Job seemed to be filled with good news.

But then the trouble started. Enemies came and stole his oxen, his donkeys, and his camels. They even killed his servants. A lightning storm came and killed his sheep. But worst of all a strong wind came and blew down the house where all his children were staying and they were all killed.

Can you imagine how sad Job must have felt when he heard all this bad news? Job's friends thought God was punishing him; even Job's wife thought Job should be angry with God for the bad things that happened.

But then Job surprised them all when he said, "Shall we accept good from God, and not trouble?"

Job knew that the good things he used to have had come from God. But he also knew that sometimes God sends bad things in our lives. God does this to teach us to depend on him and pray to him.

Did you know that sometimes God still sends bad things into the lives of his children? Sometimes God allows his children to have pain, to have sorrow, and even to suffer in accidents. But these bad things that happen to us don't mean that God doesn't love us anymore. No, God sends trouble and pain and bad things into our lives so that we may learn to pray more, and depend on God more and more for his help and care.

What will you do when trouble comes? Do like Job did and say that we can accept both the good and the bad things because we know all things come from God. He sends us what he knows is best for us. He sends us what we need to keep us close to him.

Remember to thank God when your life is filled with good things and pray for his help when bad things come.

31

Jeremiah

Concept: God has power over all people and
    nations
Object: Modeling clay
Text: Jeremiah 18:6

*Like clay in the hand of the potter, so are you in my
hand, O house of Israel.*

Do you like to play with modeling clay? *(Allow
responses.)* Or maybe you have made things with real
clay in art class at school. You can squeeze it into all
kinds of shapes like this. *(Demonstrate.)* Who would
like to make the lump of clay look nice and round
like a baseball? *(Allow one child to form the clay like a
baseball and show the class.)* Thank you. Now who
would like to change the shape so it looks like a football? *(Choose another child to use the same clay to form
a football shape. Have the child show the class; praise
the work done, and take the clay back.)*

You know that you can take the same lump of clay
and make many different things from it. In a factory
where clay is molded, part of a large lump of clay
could be made into a beautiful lamp but another part
of the same large lump could be made into an ordi-
nary wastebasket.

The clay can't say to the potter—that's what they call a person who makes things out of clay—"Make me into a beautiful lamp; I don't want to be made into a wastebasket!" No, the potter just takes a piece of clay and makes what he wants to make.

Long ago God wanted to send a message to his people Israel. So he told his prophet, Jeremiah, to go to a potter's house. There Jeremiah saw the potter busy at work shaping a pot. But the pot he was trying to make didn't turn out right, so he squeezed the clay together and made another pot from the same clay but in a different shape.

God told the prophet Jeremiah to tell the people of Israel to stop doing evil things. God said if the Israelites didn't obey him he would punish them instead of bless them.

God could do this because he is the almighty ruler of heaven and earth. God can still send blessings or troubles to our nation today. He still watches over the world to see if people obey his Word.

But God doesn't just watch over the countries of the world; he watches over each one of us, too. He sends both blessings and troubles into our lives to mold us and make us into the kind of persons he wants us to be.

There is a song that says,

> *"mold me and make me, after Thy will,*
> *while I am waiting, yielded and still."*

(Hold up the clay football.) The clay can't complain if we make it into the shape of a baseball or football.

Remember that when God sends troubles into our lives to squeeze us into the kind of person he wants us to be, we shouldn't complain either. Instead we need to thank God for his love and care for us. *(Have the congregation sing, "Have Thine Own Way, Lord" as the children return to their seats.)*

32

Daniel

Concept: The importance of prayer
Object: Picture of a lion
Texts: Daniel 6:11, 16

Then these men . . . found Daniel praying. . . . and they brought Daniel and threw him into the lions' den.

How many of you have ever been to the zoo and seen a real live lion? Good, or maybe you saw pictures of real lions on a TV program. I brought a picture of a lion to show you today. *(Do so—and point out a few features such as strong muscles and large teeth.)* Maybe some of you have even heard a lion growl or roar!

The Bible tells us a story about lions. Long ago when Daniel lived, King Nebuchadnezzar kept lions in a den. A den is a place something like a cave. They kept a big stone over the opening of the den so the lions couldn't get out. Then, when they had some wicked men that they wanted to punish, instead of putting them in jail like we do today, they put them in the lions' den and the lions killed them and ate them up.

Daniel served the king but he didn't pray to the king because he loved and trusted God. He prayed to God three times a day. Some other wicked people who hated Daniel knew this. They went to the king and asked him to make a law that whoever prayed to anybody except the king would be thrown into the lions' den.

Do you think this made Daniel stop praying to God? *(Allow responses.)* Right! Daniel prayed to God just like he always did. So they threw Daniel into the den of lions. But God shut the lions' mouths so they couldn't hurt Daniel. What a wonderful story about how God took care of Daniel.

Praying was really important to Daniel. He didn't stop praying even though he knew he would be thrown into the lions' den if he did. Is praying to God that important to you? Let's always remember to pray like Daniel did!

33

Jonah

Concept: Going the right way
Object: A sign that says "one way"
Text: Jonah 1:3

But Jonah ran away from the LORD . . . he found a ship . . . After paying the fare, he went aboard and sailed for Tarshish to flee from the LORD.

How many of you know what this sign says? *(Allow responses.)* Right. And the arrow shows which direction you have to go. If you were riding in a car and the driver went the wrong way, you could have a bad wreck.

In the Bible, in the Book of Jonah, there is a story of a man who went the wrong way. God told Jonah to go to the city of Nineveh to tell the people that if they didn't repent, God would destroy the city in forty days.

So what did Jonah do? Do you think that he did what God told him to do? *(Allow responses.)*

Jonah bought a ticket and got on a boat that was going to Tarshish. He tried to go west instead of east. *(Point in the two directions.)* He was going the wrong way. But he had a wreck. It wasn't a wreck with a car. Instead God sent a great storm and the other sailors threw Jonah into the sea. Then God sent a great fish to swallow Jonah.

From inside the great fish, Jonah prayed to God and the fish brought Jonah back to the shore and vomited him up onto dry land.

Then God called Jonah a second time and told him to go to preach to the people of Nineveh. This time Jonah went the right way. He went to the city and proclaimed the news that if the people did not repent, God would destroy Nineveh in forty days.

The people of Nineveh listened to Jonah. They showed God how sorry they were for their sins by fasting and by wearing sackcloth—a hard rough cloth—instead of their regular clothes. They also gave up their evil ways of living just as the king of Nineveh asked them to do.

Then God showed how merciful and forgiving he is. God forgave their sins and spared the city. The story of Jonah shows us once again how great the love of God is. It also shows us how important it is for us to go the right way. *(Point to the sign.)*

Let's all be sure we are going the way that God wants us to go.

34

John the Baptist

Concept: It means something to be called a Christian

Object: Chart of names with meanings

Texts: Matthew 3:1–2; Acts 11:26c

In those days John the Baptist came, preaching in the Desert of Judea and saying, "Repent, for the kingdom of heaven is near."

The disciples were called Christians first at Antioch.

Boys and girls, this is a chart of some names with their meanings. *(Include names such as the following:)*

Ann—graceful
Daniel—God is my judge
Joel—the Lord is God
Megan—strong or great
Rachel—innocent

Many years ago the Indian people gave names that had special meaning to their children. For example, a boy might be named Running Deer. Why do you think he might be called by that name? *(Allow responses.)*

History tells us about a man that others called

Richard, the Lion-hearted. Can you imagine why he got that name? *(Allow responses.)* Richard was a brave leader in the army. The name people used when they talked about this man tells us something about the kind of person he was.

Look at my chart and you will see that many names have special meanings. *(Read a few and give their meanings.)* Did you know that some people study names to tell how they got started and what they mean? For example, many people today have the last name of Johnson. It started a long time ago when they called a boy "John's son" because his father's name was John. That's how names like Peterson and Jackson got started too.

Some people got their names from what they did. Mr. Harper was a man who played the harp. Mr. Farmer was a man who lived on a farm.

The Bible tells us about a man called John the Baptist or John the Baptizer. God gave him a special job to do. He had to tell the people that Jesus, the Savior, was coming soon. So John preached near the Jordan River, "Repent of your sins, and be baptized." When people said they were sorry for their sins, John the Baptist baptized them in the water of the river. He got them ready for the time when Jesus would appear to them.

After Jesus Christ had died on the cross, had risen from the grave and gone back to heaven, Jesus Christ's disciples went to many places telling others to follow him too. Other people noticed how the followers of Jesus Christ lived like Jesus wanted them to and how they loved one another; they called them Christians. What a wonderful name to have!

But to be called a Christian, you have to be a follower of Christ. The people of the city said that the Christians were turning the world upside down because they wanted to do things differently—they tried to live the way Jesus wanted them to live.

Are you ashamed when people call you a Christian? Or are you happy when people call you by that name? Always remember to try to be like Jesus so others can see that you really are a Christian.

35

Philip

Concept: Bringing others to Jesus

Object: Picture of something that is special to you

Text: John 1:46b

"Come and see," said Philip.

Today I'd like to begin by showing you a picture of something that is really special to me. *(Show the children a picture of a pet, a special machine or tool, an antique, or something that is too big or inappropriate to bring to the class. Answer questions they may have about the object pictured.)*

Some of you may have something that's really important to you like a special game, a special model airplane, or a special picture. When you try to tell your friends about it, it may be that you can't find the right words to describe it, or maybe your friends won't believe you. If you really want your friends to believe what you said about your special thing, what's the best thing to do? *(Allow responses.)* You need to invite your friends to come to see that special thing you have and when they see it, they will believe you.

A long time ago when Jesus was on earth, as he began his public ministry he called together twelve disciples. One of the first disciples Jesus called was Philip. Philip was so glad he had found the Messiah. He was so excited about knowing the Savior God had promised, that he went quickly to find his friend, Nathanael, to tell him about Jesus.

But Nathanael wouldn't believe Philip. Then Philip said something that is very important for us to remember. He said, "Come and see!"

Nathanael did that. He came with Philip to see Jesus. Then Nathanael believed in Jesus and became a disciple just like Philip was. When Philip said, "Come and see," he said just the right thing. He invited Nathanael to meet Jesus.

If you are excited about being a Christian and you really like your church and Sunday school, you will want to do what Philip did—talk about them to others. Then when they ask more about what you do there, just say, "Come and see," like Philip did. Invite them to come to know Jesus.

Whenever you find someone who isn't a Christian, invite that person to come to church with you so they can find out for themselves what a very special person Jesus really is—the Son of God and the Savior of the world.

36

Nathanael

Concept: Jesus sees us wherever we are
Object: Picture of a tree house
Text: John 1:48

Jesus answered, "I saw you while you were still under the fig tree before Philip called you."

Today I would like to show you this picture of a tree house. Let me tell you a little bit about it. *(At this point you could describe the ladder or steps used to get up to it, the way you can look down out of the windows, etc.)* Have any of you ever been in a tree house? *(Allow responses. A few may say they have been in a tree house; if so, ask them a few questions about it. If no one has been in a real tree house, ask if anyone has seen a tree house on TV. At that point you will likely get several responses.)*

One of the nice things about a tree house is that it can be something like a secret hiding place. If your living room is noisy and the TV is on, you may just want to be in a quiet place and read for a while. Or after a busy time with your friends, you may just want to be by yourself in a spot that you enjoy.

The Bible tells us about a man named Nathanael. At the time that Nathanael lived, houses had few rooms; in fact, many had only one big room. It was pretty hard for a person to find a quiet spot to be by himself.

But Nathanael had found a favorite spot under a big fig tree. Such big old trees often had branches that stretched out and hung down to the ground. Inside that circle of limbs and leaves, Nathanael had found a quiet spot to be alone.

Nathanael's tree house wasn't up in the tree like most tree houses today. It was on the ground, hidden under the stretched out branches of the tree.

When Nathanael first came to Jesus, Jesus said, "I saw you while you were still under the fig tree before Philip called you." Jesus saw Nathanael even in his special hiding place.

Nathanael was really surprised that Jesus could see him in his hiding place. Suddenly Nathanael knew that Jesus was God, for only God can always see you.

The Bible tells us that the eyes of the Lord are everywhere. He sees all that we do. We are never out of his sight.

Isn't that wonderful! Let's always try to remember that wherever we are we are always in God's loving, watchful care.

37

The Boy with Five Loaves and Two Fish

Concept: The importance of sharing
Object: Lunch bucket with cookies to share
Text: John 6:9

Here is a boy with five small barley loaves and two small fish, but how far will they go among so many?

This is my lunch bucket, girls and boys. Because I can't go home from work at noon, I have to take my lunch along with me. Then when it's noontime I just open it up and see what's inside for me to eat.

Do any of you take a lunch along with you to school in a paper bag or lunch bucket? *(Allow responses. You may also wish to ask if their parents or brothers or sisters take a lunch along to work or school.)*

Well, it seems that most of us know what a lunch bucket is for. We use it to take food to school or to work when we can't go home for a meal. It's fun to open your lunch bucket at recess time to get a snack and peek to see what your Mom put inside for your noon lunch, isn't it?

One day a boy went to school but he forgot to take his lunch bucket along. Then when lunch time came, the teacher noticed he didn't have anything to eat. The teacher asked if any of the other boys and girls would like to share something with that boy who didn't have a lunch. Then the other children began to share. From one he got a peanut butter and jelly sandwich, from another he got a cookie; someone else gave him an apple, and soon he had more than enough to eat.

There is a story in the Bible about a boy who had two small fish and five barley loaves with him when he went to follow Jesus. The boy was not the only person following Jesus. There was a huge crowd of five thousand and they were all getting hungry.

When Jesus asked his disciples to feed the people, the only food they could find was the two small fish and five small loaves of bread that the boy had. Then Jesus worked a wonderful miracle.

Jesus asked all the people to sit down on the grass. He gave thanks to God for the food and then he shared it with the people. All of those thousands of people had enough to eat from one little boy's lunch. They even had twelve baskets of food left over.

We can't do a miracle like Jesus did. But we can share what we have like the little boy did. There are so many hungry people in the world. Because we love Jesus, let's do all we can to give them the food they need to stay alive and be healthy and happy.

Before you go back to your seats, I think we should look in my lunch bucket, don't you? *(Open it.)* Look, it's full of cookies! I think we should share these so that you can remember to share what you have with others too. *(Give each child a cookie as they go back to their seats, or if this is not appropriate in your setting, invite them to get one from you after the church service.)*

The Woman Who Touched Jesus' Robe and Was Healed

Concept: Having faith in Jesus
Object: A robe
Text: Mark 5:28

She thought, "If I just touch his clothes, I will be healed."

Girls and boys, do you notice that I'm dressed differently this morning? *(Allow responses.)* I wore my robe for a very special reason. I wore it because the lesson this morning is about Jesus' robe. Long ago when Jesus was on earth, the men usually wore robes as their main article of clothing.

Jesus had a robe that was woven of one piece of material. It didn't have seams with parts sewed together like this one does. *(Show the girls and boys where the seams in your robe are.)*

At that time Jesus walked from place to place, from city to city, in the land of Palestine. His disciples followed him and sometimes large crowds of people joined them. When sick people came to Jesus, he would heal them. Jesus could do this because he was God.

One day a woman who had been sick for twelve years heard that Jesus was coming. She had been to many doctors, but no one seemed to be able to help her. She decided to go to Jesus and ask if he would heal her.

But as she came to where Jesus was, she saw the crowd. There were people all around him. She wondered how she could ask Jesus to heal her with so many people there.

Then she had an idea. Maybe she wouldn't have to ask him to heal her. She believed that Jesus was so powerful that if she could just touch him, she would be healed.

So she started toward the crowd—toward Jesus. Everyone was pushing and shoving, trying to get close to where Jesus was. She squirmed and worked her way through the crowd and gradually got closer. Finally she was close enough. She reached out and touched Jesus' robe.

At that very instant, she knew the sickness in her body was healed. She was all better! How wonderful after all those years of sickness and going to doctors!

Then something quite frightening happened! Jesus stopped walking. He asked, "Who touched my clothes?" The disciples thought it was only someone in the crowd who had pushed against Jesus. But Jesus knew it was someone special.

Jesus saw the woman who had been healed. She came and kneeled at Jesus' feet and told him what she had done. Jesus said, "Daughter, your faith has healed you. Go in peace and be freed from your suffering."

Isn't that wonderful, girls and boys! Jesus said, "Your faith has healed you!" Do you know what faith is? Faith is trusting and really believing in Jesus.

The sick woman came to Jesus along the road in the middle of a crowd of people. We can come to Jesus too, every time we pray. When we ask Jesus for help, we can't reach out and touch his robe, but we do need faith just like the sick woman needed faith. When we really believe, Jesus will answer our prayers and fill our needs just like he filled the need of the sick woman. Jesus is always the same, yesterday, today, and forever. He can answer our prayers just as easily as he could heal the woman who touched the hem of his robe. Let's always remember that when we pray.

39

Zaccheus

Concept: Jesus came to seek and to save the lost

Object: A step stool

Text: Luke 19:10

For the Son of Man came to seek and to save what was lost.

Who knows what a step stool can be used for? *(Allow responses.)* Right! If you weren't quite big enough to reach a cookie out of the cookie jar on the countertop, and if your Mom said it was OK, you could put the step stool in the right place, stand up on it, and you would be big enough to reach a cookie. *(Demonstrate by stepping up on the step stool.)*

A step stool could help you too if you wanted to look out of a window that was just a little too high up for you to look out. You just step up on your stool and there you are, big enough to see what you wanted to see. If you're tall, you don't need a step stool, because you can look over the heads of everybody else, but if you're short, a step stool can really come in handy.

The Bible tells us about a little man named Zacchaeus who wanted to see Jesus. Wherever Jesus went large crowds of people would be around him. But when Zacchaeus tried to see Jesus, it seemed like somebody bigger and taller was always standing in front of him.

Then Zacchaeus had an idea. He didn't have a step stool, so he ran ahead of the crowd and climbed up in a tree along the road. That was even better than a step stool. Then he waited for Jesus to come walking by. At last he would get to see Jesus.

Well, Jesus did walk by on the road under the tree that Zacchaeus had climbed. He even stopped under the tree, looked up right into the face of the little man who didn't have a step stool and he said, "Zacchaeus, come down, I must stay at your house today."

How did Jesus know that Zacchaeus was up in the tree? Jesus knows everything, because Jesus is the Son of God.

Well, Jesus did go to the house of Zacchaeus. He brought salvation to his family and Zacchaeus promised to give half of what he owned to the poor. He also promised Jesus that if he had cheated anybody, he would give back four times as much as he had taken.

Jesus knew that Zacchaeus was a sinful man. But that didn't keep Jesus from going to Zacchaeus's house and forgiving his sins. The Bible tells us that Jesus came to seek and to save lost sinners. That's why Jesus died on the cross.

Whenever you climb on a step stool to reach a little higher, or to look over the top of something, think of that little man, Zacchaeus. Remember, too, that Jesus loved him and he also loves you.

40

Thomas

Concept: Proof of Jesus' resurrection
Object: Scars
Text: John 20:27

Then he said to Thomas, "Put your finger here; see my hands. Reach out your hand and put it into my side. Stop doubting and believe."

Girls and boys, would you look at this? *(Show a scar that you have, or get someone else to show a scar.)* The skin looks a little different, doesn't it? We call marks like this scars. A scar shows that the skin healed up again after it was cut or scratched. How many of you have a scar? *(Allow responses. Select one child with an elbow or knee scar to tell what happened, or tell what happened to cause your scar.)*

Isn't it wonderful that God makes it possible for cuts and scratches to heal up again? If we get a new wagon for a Christmas or birthday present and the paint gets a big scratch, it can't heal up again; only living things can do that.

The scratch or cut may heal up, but the scar is there to help us remember what happened.

The Bible tells us about some very important scars. They are the scars in the hands, feet, and side of Jesus.

When the Roman soldiers crucified Jesus, they drove nails in his hands and feet. To find out if Jesus had really died, a Roman soldier stuck a spear in his side.

After Jesus rose from the grave on Easter morning, he came to his disciples to show them that he was alive again. All the disciples were there except Thomas.

When the other disciples told Thomas what had happened he wouldn't believe that Jesus had really risen from the dead because he hadn't seem him.

Thomas said, "Unless I see the nail marks in his hands and put my finger where the nails were, and put my hand into his side, I will not believe it." He wanted to see Jesus' scars.

A week later Jesus suddenly appeared to his disciples again. This time Thomas was with them. Jesus invited Thomas to come and touch his scars. Then Thomas knew it was really Jesus.

Jesus said to Thomas, "Because you have seen me, you have believed; blessed are those who have not seen and yet have believed." Because Thomas doubted and saw Jesus' scars, we have another proof that Jesus really did rise from the grave and truly is alive again.

When you look at your scars, you can remember what happened to cause them, but do one more thing. Think about Jesus' scars and then remember that he died on the cross to save you from your sins.

James the Son of Alphaeus

Concept: Silent followers of Jesus
Object: Sign with the word QUIET
Text: Matthew 10:3

James the son of Alphaeus. . . .

Girls and boys, do you know what this means? *(Place your index finger over your mouth and say "Shhh." Allow responses.)* And what do you suppose this sign says? *(Hold up the "QUIET" sign.)*

When do we have to be quiet? *(Allow responses.)*

Some people find it easy to talk a lot, but other people are more quiet. When nobody is talking, we sometimes say that it is silent. *(You may wish to have the children say this word together.)*

Today I would like to tell you about one of Jesus' disciples. His name was James. Jesus had two disciples called James. One was a real leader. Jesus called him a "son of thunder." But the other James, James the son of Alphaeus, was a quiet follower of Jesus. This James followed Jesus for three years and later became an apostle but the Bible doesn't tell us one question that this James asked or one word that he said. That's why we sometimes call him the "silent follower of Jesus."

Today Jesus still has a lot of silent followers. They just quietly do the work of God's kingdom even though nobody seems to notice. They don't get a lot of praise for what they do; in fact, others may not even know about what they do for Jesus. But Jesus knows and Jesus cares.

Remember that in God's kingdom it's important to tell others about Jesus like Peter and John did. But it's also very important that Jesus' silent followers do God's will and God's work in all sorts of quiet ways. That's how James, son of Alphaeus, showed that he loved Jesus and that's how we can show Jesus that we love him too.

42

Simon the Zealot

Concept: Being enthusiastic for God's kingdom

Objects: A cheerleader's pompon and a picture of fans cheering at a ball game

Text: Matthew 10:4

Simon the Zealot . . .

How many of you know what this is for? *(Wave the pompon and allow responses.)* Yes, they wave pompons up and down and all around *(demonstrate),* and they lead the crowd in cheering for the basketball or football team. Some of them kick up their legs or turn somersaults, but I can't show you how they do that!

Here's a picture of the crowd at a ball game. Look at all the people standing up and cheering for their team! Maybe you have watched a ball game on television and have seen people cheering for their favorite team.

People who cheer for their favorite team this way are called *fans,* a word that comes from fanatic. It means they have a lot of enthusiasm or zeal for their team.

A long time ago, when Jesus was on earth, he chose twelve disciples to be his followers. One of the

113

twelve was Simon the Zealot. He was called the Zealot because he had a lot of zeal for his country. He wanted Israel to be free from the rule of Rome. The zealots did all they could in secret ways to fight against the Romans. They had a lot of enthusiasm for the kingdom of Israel.

As Christians we are all servants of the King of Kings. We should have as much enthusiasm for our heavenly king as the zealots did for the earthly kingdom of Israel that they wanted to establish.

How happy and eager are you to be here at _____ Church today? Do you have so much zeal for Jesus that you just can't wait to tell others about him?

When other people saw Simon, they noticed how enthusiastic he was; how filled with zeal for the kingdom of Israel. It was so noticeable that they called him Simon the Zealot.

When other people see you and me, can they tell we are eager and enthusiastic about serving Jesus? Would they call you *(use a few of the children's names)* _____ the Zealot? People should be able to see that we love Jesus by how eager we are to serve him. Let's try to let our love for Jesus bubble over so everyone can really see that we love him.

43

Pontius Pilate

Concept: Only Jesus' blood can cleanse us from sin

Objects: A basin of water, a bar of soap, a towel, a water-soluble marker to mark one hand, and a permanent marker to mark the other

Text: Matthew 27:24

Pilate . . . took water and washed his hands in front of the crowd. "I am innocent of this man's blood," he said. "It is your responsibility!"

How many of you always remember to wash your hands when they're dirty? *(Allow responses.)* Do your moms or dads ever tell you to wash your hands, maybe after you played in the sandbox, and before supper? It's sometimes hard to remember that we should wash our hands after we go to the bathroom or before we eat, isn't it? Then our parents remind us until we are so grown-up we can remember all by ourselves. When we wash our hands, most dirt comes off easily, but to get some dirt off, you really have to scrub. *(Demonstrate by showing your hands to the class; then wash them and show how one readily becomes clean while the other doesn't. Apply some soap and really rub the one hand marked with the permanent marker and show how it just doesn't want to get clean.)*

In the Bible, girls and boys, there is a story about a man who asked for a basin of water to wash his hands. That man's name was Pontius Pilate.

It happened when the Jewish leaders brought Jesus to be condemned to death. The Jews shouted "Crucify him! Crucify him!" Pontius Pilate was the Roman ruler. He knew that the Jews hated Jesus. He also knew that Jesus was not guilty of doing any wrong so Pilate tried to set Jesus free.

What could Pilate do? If he didn't do what the Jewish leaders said, it would seem as if he was going against Caesar and the government of Rome. If he didn't crucify Jesus, the Jews might start a riot or an uproar. If he did what the Jewish leaders wanted he would be to blame for crucifying an innocent person.

Then Pilate had an idea. He would ask his servant to bring a basin of water and he would wash his hands in front of the people and blame them for the whole problem. "I am innocent of this man's blood," he said. "It is your responsibility."

Pilate thought he could blame somebody else for doing what he knew was wrong. But that doesn't work. The wrong thing that Pilate did stained his hands and the stain wouldn't wash off just like the marks on this hand. *(Hold up the hand you marked with the permanent marker.)*

No, we can't blame someone else for the wrong things we do. And we can't wash them away ourselves. There is just one thing that can take away our sins and that's the blood of Jesus. His blood cleanses us from all our sins. Let's remember to thank him for that!

Ananias and Sapphira

Concept: God knows all of our thoughts
Object: An exposed X-ray film
Text: 1 Samuel 16:7b

The LORD does not look at the things man looks at. Man looks at the outward appearance, but the LORD looks at the heart.

Let's begin today by looking at our hands. *(Stretch out your hands and look at them.)* What do you see? *(Allow responses.)* When we look at our hands we see our thumbs and fingers and we see the skin that God made to cover them. But what do you think is under the skin? *(Allow responses.)* We know that there must be bones because we can feel something hard inside. *(Demonstrate by pinching your hands and fingers.)* And we know that there must be muscles inside because muscles help us to move. *(Demonstrate by flexing fingers.)* If we fall and cut or scratch our skin we bleed, so we know that there is blood under the skin. But we can't see what's inside by looking at the outside.

Did you know that doctors can take a picture with a machine called an X-ray machine? This X-ray machine can take a picture of your bones right through your skin. If the doctor thinks you have a

118

broken bone, he can take a picture like this one. *(Show the X-ray picture.)* Can you see the bones in the picture? It's hard to believe but the X-ray machine can see the bones inside of you by taking a picture from outside of your body. But God is greater than all the X-ray machines in the world. God knows more than just where all your bones are, he even knows everything you think about in your mind.

The Bible tells us about a man named Ananias and his wife Sapphira who lived a long time ago. They decided to sell their land and give some money to the church. But they wanted to keep some of the money themselves. That was fine except for one thing.

They decided to tell the apostle Peter that they were giving *all* their money to the church. They decided together to tell a lie about the money they wanted to keep.

First Ananias brought the money and laid it at the apostle's feet. He lied when he told Peter that it was all the money they had gotten for the land they sold. But God knew it was a lie and Ananias was punished. He died right there.

A little later Sapphira came to the apostle Peter. Peter asked her if the money Ananias brought was all the money they had gotten for the land. Then Sapphira told the same lie her husband, Ananias, had told. God could see into her heart too. God knew she had told a lie and God punished her in the same way. She died too.

The bones inside your skin can't hide when the doctor takes an X-ray picture of your hand. And you

119

can't hide any of your thoughts from God. He knows when you think bad things. He knows when you think good things.

Remember to be careful what you think. If you think a bad thought, get a good thought to push it out of your mind. When you look at your skin, remember that God doesn't just look at the outside, he sees the inside too; God knows everything.

45

Stephen

Concept: Forgiving others
Objects: Several coats and/or sweaters
Text: Acts 7:60

Lord, do not hold this sin against them.

Girls and boys, what do you think happens when you run fast and play hard? *(Allow responses.)* And what do you do if you get too warm? *(Allow responses.)* Right. *(Demonstrate by taking off your outer coat.)* And if you play some more and start to sweat, what do you do next? *(Allow responses.)* Right. *(Demonstrate again by taking off one or two sweaters.)*

I guess boys and girls and even older people take off their coats and sweaters when they play or work hard. Did you know that there is a story in the Bible about some people who took off their coats and laid them on a pile at the feet of Saul who later became a great missionary?

The reason these people took their coats off was because they were angry with Stephen. Stephen was a Christian. He loved Jesus. The same Jews who wanted Jesus crucified now wanted to kill Jesus' followers.

After Stephen told the Jews that Jesus was the Messiah, the Savior of the world, they became very angry. They dragged Stephen out of the city to kill him with stones. They were so angry they took off their coats so they could throw the stones even harder.

Think of Stephen. The angry crowd was throwing stones at him. If you have ever gotten hit with a stone by accident, you know how much it hurts. The men throwing stones at Stephen didn't hit him by accident; they tried to hit him on purpose. They threw the stones as hard as they could. That's why they took off their coats.

But even in his pain, Stephen did a very special thing. He asked God to forgive the sins of those who were throwing the stones at him! Where do you think Stephen had learned how to forgive others, even people who were doing bad things to him? *(Allow responses.)* Stephen learned how to forgive from Jesus. When people do bad things to you, remember that Jesus wants us to forgive others just like he forgives us. Stephen did; let's try to do it too.

The Apostle Paul

Concept: Although we give away the gospel, we still keep it

Objects: A small toy, three candles, and two adult volunteers

Text: Mark 16:15

Go into all the world and preach the good news to all creation.

Look at this toy I brought, girls and boys. *(Describe it.)* Now I want to pass the toy to _____ *(Choose a boy or girl near you.)* Do I still have the toy? *(Allow responses.)* Now let's ask _____ to hand it to _____ (another boy or girl). Who has it now? *(Allow responses.)* Now I'd like to ask _____ (child who has toy) to pass it back to me. Did you notice that only one person at a time could have the toy? As soon as I gave it to _____ I didn't have it anymore. And when _____ (1st child) gave it to _____ (2nd child), _____ (1st child) didn't have it anymore.

I'd like to have you look at this candle. *(Take one and light it carefully.)* The flame is burning brightly, isn't it? Next, let's give another candle to _____ (1st adult) and one to _____ (2nd adult). First I will light

123

_____'s (1st adult) candle; then _____ he/she can light _____'s (2nd adult) candle.

Look at the three candles. Did my candle go out because I gave some of the flame to _____? (1st adult). Did _____'s (1st adult) candle go out because he/she gave some of the flame to _____ (2nd adult)? *(Allow responses.)* Right, the candles stayed burning just as brightly even though some of the flame was given away.

Let's put the candles away now because I want to tell you about the apostle Paul. The Bible tells us about him because he was one of the greatest missionaries that ever lived. Paul brought the good news of Jesus to many, many people. He went on missionary journeys to many countries. Everywhere Paul went he told people about Jesus.

Giving the good news about Jesus to others isn't like giving a toy away. When you give the toy away, you don't have it anymore; someone else has it instead.

Paul showed us that giving the good news about Jesus to others is more like lighting someone else's candle. Your own candle still burns just as brightly as it did before you gave away some of the flame.

When the apostle Paul brought the gospel to others, he even learned to love and serve Jesus more himself.

You can do that too. When you tell others about Jesus, you don't have to be afraid that you won't have the Good News anymore yourself. Remember that you can give away the Good News, but you'll always still have it for yourself.

King Agrippa

Concept: Being "almost" a Christian is not enough

Object: A large sign with the word **ALMOST** on it

Text: Acts 26:28 (KJV)

Then Agrippa said unto Paul, "Almost thou persuadest me to be a Christian."

Girls and boys, I have a very important word to show you this morning. *(Hold up your sign.)* Some of you may know it already; it's the word *almost*. Let's say it together, "almost." Once again, "almost."

We use this word lots of times. Let me try a few. Suppose there was a cookie on the table that you wanted. Then suppose you would try to reach it but you weren't quite tall enough even if you stretched your arm up as far as you could and stood on your tiptoes. Then you would say "I'm **almost** tall enough to reach it."

Or suppose you went fishing and a big fish came swimming by, but instead of biting on your hook, he just looked at it and swam away. You could say, "Well, I **almost** caught a big fish."

Or maybe you were running a race and you were tied with another runner. Then just as you were getting to the end of the race, the other runner dashed ahead to the finish line. You could say, "Well, I **almost** won the race."

We use this word *(point to **almost** sign)* lots of times. We sometimes say, "I'm **almost** ready for church," or "The TV program is **almost** over," or "I **almost** know how to swim."

But if I say "I **almost** know how to swim," I better not jump into a deep swimming pool because **almost** isn't enough. If I say, "I **almost** caught the school bus," it means I really missed it. Again, **almost** isn't enough. I have to be on time to catch it.

In the Bible there is a story about a man who said, **almost**. That man's name was King Agrippa. The great missionary, Paul, told King Agrippa how to become a Christian. The King **almost** believed Paul. He **almost** became a Christian and began to love Jesus. **Almost**, but not quite.

That means King Agrippa didn't become a Christian at all. If you almost catch the bus, it means you missed the bus. If you almost caught a fish, it means you didn't catch a fish at all. Or if you almost did what your mother or father asked you to do, it means you didn't do what they said.

It will never work to say, "I **almost** love Jesus." That's what King Agrippa said, but it wasn't enough. Jesus doesn't want children who almost love him. He wants his children to really love him. Let's throw the ALMOST card away *(tear or wrinkle it up)* and let's really try to love Jesus with our whole heart and mind and strength.

Eutychus—the Young Man Who Slept in Church

Concept: Attentiveness in church
Object: A pillow
Text: Matthew 13:9

He who has ears, let him hear.

How do you like my pillow? *(Allow the children to touch it or put their cheeks on it.)* My pillow is nice and soft, and if I were really tired at night, I could go to bed and put my head on it. Then I would probably go to sleep quite quickly.

When you want to go to sleep, it's nice to have a soft, feathery pillow. In fact, even if you weren't sleepy at all, putting your head on a nice pillow could probably make you feel a little sleepy right here in church. *(Put your head on the pillow and yawn.)*

In the Bible, we find a story of a young man named Eutychus who did fall asleep in church. Paul was the preacher and it was a special service because Paul was there. They were meeting in an upstairs room and the sermon got longer and longer. Paul preached until midnight.

There were many lamps in the room and maybe

127

the room was warm and stuffy and Eutychus was getting sleepy. So Eutychus went to sit on a window ledge. Maybe he thought the fresh air would help to keep him awake. But it didn't and soon Eutychus wasn't listening to what Paul was preaching about; no, he was fast asleep.

And then it happened! Eutychus got relaxed. At first his head probably started to nod like this. *(Demonstrate.)* Next he got so relaxed he started to sag down a bit. *(Demonstrate again.)* But then all of a sudden, he fell right off the window ledge where he was sitting. He fell down to the ground three stories below.

The rest of the people in church rushed out and found that the fall from such a high window had killed Eutychus. But then the great apostle Paul who had done many miracles by God's power in many places, came outside. He threw himself on the young man and put his arms around him. God caused another miracle to happen. Eutychus became alive again!

The people went back inside and they celebrated the Lord's Supper together. Paul preached until morning but I don't think anyone was sleepy during the rest of the sermon.

Today some people may bring a pillow to church because they have a sore back; the pillow makes it possible for them to attend church. But most of us don't come to church with pillows to sleep on, do we?

No, we come to church to praise God, and to listen to the minister as he brings God's Word to us.

To do this we have to pay attention; and we have to be wide awake.

When God created Adam and Eve, he gave them ears so they could hear. When Jesus was on earth he said, "He that has ears, let him hear!"

That means we have to work hard to listen and try to understand God's Word. We have to be wide awake! Don't go to sleep in church like Eutychus did.

Dorcas

Concept: Showing love for Jesus by helping others

Objects: Knitted stocking caps or other hand-made articles of clothing

Text: Acts 9:39b (KJV)

All the widows stood by him weeping, and shewing the coats and garments which Dorcas made, while she was with them.

Let me show you something very special, boys and girls. This is a cap (or other article of clothing) that belongs to _____ (name of student). It was made by his/her grandmother. Do you think it took a long time or just a few minutes for her to make it? *(Allow responses.)* Yes, it must have taken quite a long time. Look, here is a pair of mittens (or some other article of clothing) that belongs to _____ (another member of your class). His/her mother (or grandmother) made this for _____ (student's name). Do you think it took quite a while for her to make this?

If your mother makes lunch or supper for you while you are just sitting watching TV, is that nicer than if someone said, "If you want something to eat, fix it yourself"?

Yes, it is nice if other people do things for us. When our mothers or grandmothers sew or knit something for us to wear, we know that they love us because they spend some of their time working for us.

The Bible tells us about a Christian lady by the name of Dorcas who lived long ago. Dorcas must have been good at sewing, but more than that, she must have been very willing to do things for others because she made coats and garments for the widows in the city of Joppa. Maybe she made clothes for herself too, but the Bible only tells us that she made things for others to wear. When she died, those who knew her were very sad.

They called the apostle Peter. By God's power, Peter raised Dorcas from the dead to be alive again so she could go right on doing things for others.

The story of Dorcas teaches us to do things unselfishly for others because we love Jesus.

Sometimes we need to stop and think how many things others do for us. They may cook meals and care for us; they may make or buy clothing for us; they may drive us to where we would like to go and they do many, many other things for us. We need to thank those who do these things for us and we need to thank Jesus for caring for us through them. Let's try to remember to do everything we can to help others too.

50

Timothy

Concept: It's a blessing to belong to the family of God

Objects: A cross-stitched or written out family tree with several generations, also a family picture

Text: 2 Timothy 1:5

I have been reminded of your sincere faith, which first lived in your grandmother Lois and in your mother Eunice and, I am persuaded, now lives in you also.

Girls and boys, this is a picture of our family. *(Hold up the family picture.)* I would like to tell you a little bit about my family today. First, I have _____ brothers and _____ sisters. And I have a husband (or wife) and _____ children. *(Identify some of these in the picture and point them out to the children.)*

And then I have (had) a father and a mother and I have (had) a grandfather and grandmother and a great-grandfather and a great-grandmother. All of these people are part of my family.

A family picture shows what the members of a family look like. It shows if they are young or old, or what color their hair is, how big they are, and so on.

Today we have another way of keeping a record

132

of the members of our family and that's through a family tree. Look at this one. *(Show girls and boys the one you brought with you.)* This is my name, and here are the names of my mother and father. These are the names of my grandparents and on the lines up here are the names of my great-grandparents.

It's nice to have a family and to know something about your parents and grandparents when they were young like you. Did you know that the Bible tells us about a number of family trees? In the first chapter of Matthew, we can find information about the family of Jesus so we know that he was born just the way that God had promised.

The Bible also tells us about a young Christian missionary whose name was Timothy. It even tells us that Timothy's mother, Eunice, and his grandmother, Lois, were Christians. Timothy learned about God from a Christian mother and grandmother. Isn't that wonderful?

It's really wonderful to have Christian parents and grandparents and other family members who love us and teach us to love Jesus. If you don't know all of your family members, you may want to ask your parents to tell you what their names are.

Now before we go back to our seats, let's all pray a little prayer of thanksgiving for giving us loving Christian families.

Dear Jesus, thank you for our fathers and mothers and all the rest of our family members. Help us all to love one another and really be part of the family of God. We pray in your name, Amen.